DIABETIC
COOKBOOK FOR
BEGINNERS

ANDREW WERDAN

Contents

INTRODUCTION

What Is Diabetes?

Diabetes Is A Long-Term (Chronic) Disease That Alters How Your Body Converts Energy From Food. Most Of The Food You Consume Is Converted Into Glucose, Then Released Into Circulation. Your Pancreas Produces Insulin When Your Blood Glucose Levels Spike. For Blood Glucose To Enter Your Body's Cells And Be Used As Energy, Insulin Functions As A Door.

When You Have Diabetes, Your Body Produces Insufficient Insulin Or Misuses It. Too Much Blood Glucose Remains In Your Circulation When Low Insulin Or Cells Cease Reacting To Insulin. That Can Eventually Lead To Significant Health Issues Like Renal Disease, Eyesight Loss, And Cardiovascular Disease.

There Is Yet To Be A Proper Cure For Diabetes, But There Are Specific Ways You Can Fight The Chronic Illness In Your Way:

- Eating Well
- Exercising and remaining active
- Taking proper medications
- Being aware of diabetes and taking appropriate measures.
- Having adequate health care appointments and opinions on it

Types of Diabetes:

Type 1:

Diabetes type 1 is a chronic illness called insulin-dependent or juvenile diabetes. The pancreas in your body produces very little or no insulin. A hormone called insulin is what the body utilizes to let glucose (sugar) into cells, where your body may use it to make energy.

There is still no cure for type 1 diabetes, despite much research. The goal of the treatment is to avoid problems by regulating blood sugar levels with insulin, food, and lifestyle modification.

Various reasons, including genetics and some viruses, may bring on type 1 diabetes. While type 1 diabe- tes often manifests in infancy or youth, it can also strike adults.

Symptoms:

Symptoms consist of but are not limited to:

- Being thirstier than normal
- A great deal of urination
- Infants who've never soaked their bed at night develop bedwetting
- shedding pounds without trying
- Experiencing irritability or other mood swings
- Being worn out and fragile
- Having eyesight haze

Type 2:

A disorder in the body's ability to control and utilize glucose (sugar) as energy is type 2 diabetes. This continuous (long-term) disorder causes the bloodstream to circulate with an excessive amount of sugar. Over time, cardiovascular, neurological, and immune system issues might result from excessive blood sugar levels.

There are two interconnected issues at play in type 2 diabetes. The hormone that controls the flow of glucose into your tissues, insulin, is not produced by your pancreas in sufficient amounts, which causes your cells to react negatively to insulin and absorb less glucose.

Although type 1 and 2 diabetes may start in infancy and adulthood, type 2 diabetes was previously classified as adult-onset diabetes. Although type 2 is more prevalent in elderly persons, type 2 instances have increased in younger generations due to the rise in childhood obesity.

Although there is no treatment for type two diabetes, you may moderate the condition by decreasing weight, eating healthfully, and exercising. You may also require diabetic drugs or insulin treatment to

control your blood sugar if diet and physical activity are insufficient.

Symptoms

Type 2 diabetes symptoms and signs frequently appear gradually. You may have type 2 diabetes

for de- cades without realizing it. When evident, symptoms and indications often include:
- Heightened thirst
- Often urinating
- Greater appetite
- Unwanted loss of weight
- Lethargy
- Distorted vision
- Slowly heaving wounds
- Many infections
- Tingling or numbness in the arms or legs
- Regions of skin that have browned, typically around the neck and armpits

Gestational Diabetes:

When your body can't generate sufficient insulin while you're pregnant, you get gestational diabetes. Your pancreas produces the hormone insulin, which functions as a key to allow blood glucose to reach your body's tissues to be utilized as fuel.

Your body produces additional hormones during pregnancy and other alterations like weight growth. Insulin resistance is a disorder where your body's cells absorb insulin less efficiently due to these modifi- cations. Your body requires more insulin if you have insulin resistance.

In stages of pregnancy, insulin resistance is common in pregnant women. However, some females al- ready have insulin resistance before conception. They require more significant insulin at the beginning of pregnancy and are far more likely to develop gestational diabetes.

Symptoms:

Usually, gestational diabetes has no symptoms. Your physician may believe that you have gestational diabetes based on your health information and if you possess specific health risks, but you must be ex- amined to be positive.

Best Foods for Diabetics:

Eating a range of nutritious meals from all food categories in the proportions recommended by your diet plan is essential to eating when dealing with diabetes:
- Vegetables

Non-starchy foods include tomatoes, peppers, greens, celery, and carrot. Starchy foods include green peas, potatoes, and maize.
- Fruits:

Citrus fruits, melons, grapes, bananas, apples, and berries are among the fruits.
- Grains

you should consume a minimum of half of the day's worth of grains as whole grains. Foods contain qui- noa, wheat, maize, barley, cornmeal, and oats. Others include tortillas, bread, spaghetti, and porridge.
- Protein
- Fatty meat and without skin: chicken or turkey.
- Fish
- Nuts
- Dried peas and some beans, including split peas and chickpeas. Other replacements for meat, like tofu, can work.
- Nonfat or reduced dairy

If you have a dairy sensitivity, drink milk or lactose-free milk. Yogurt and Cheese are good foods to con- sume.

Worst Foods for Diabetics:

As a person with diabetes, there may be many foods tempting enough to consume every time you are near a fast food chain or considering ordering takeout. However, there are some foods you should try not to consume ever so often.

Here are some foods you should avoid:
- Grains that have been processed, like white flour or rice.
- Cereals that are packed with glucose and low in complete grains
- Sliced bread
- Fried potatoes
- White-flour tortillas fried
- Veggies in cans with a lot of sodium added
- Veggies that have been prepared with a lot of cream, Cheese, or sauces
- Pickles when you need to reduce your salt intake. Pickles are suitable elsewhere.
- Fixes for the same purpose as sauerkraut. If you

suffer from elevated blood pressure, try to avoid them.

- Fruit in cans with a lot of sugar syrup
- Durable fruit rolls
- Average preserves, jams, and jelly
- Flavored fruit sauces
- Fruit drinks, fruit punch, and fruit juice beverages
- Chicken wings

- Higher-fat beef pieces, like ribs
- Pig bacon
- Normal Cheese
- Chicken with skin
- Fried fish in oil
- Tofu deep-fried
- Beans cooked in grease

Food glycemic index table:

Food	GI	Serving Size
Peanuts	14	4 oz (113g)
Bean sprouts	25	1 cup (104g)
Grapefruit	25	1/2 large (166g)
Pizza	30	2 slices (260g)
Low-fat yogurt	33	1 cup (245g)
Apples	38	1 medium (138g)
Spaghetti	42	1 cup (140g)
Carrots	47	1 large (72g)
Oranges	48	1 medium (131g)
Bananas	52	1 large (136g)
Potato chips	54	4 oz (114g)
Snickers Bar	55	1 bar (113g)
Brown rice	55	1 cup (195g)
Honey	55	1 tbsp (21g)
Oatmeal	58	1 cup (234g)
Ice cream	61	1 cup (72g)
Macaroni and Cheese	64	1 serving (166g)
Raisins	64	1 small box (43g)
White rice	64	1 cup (186g)
Sugar (sucrose)	68	1 tbsp (12g)
White bread	70	1 slice (30g)
Watermelon	72	1 cup (154g)
Popcorn	72	2 cups (16g)
Baked potato	85	1 medium (173g)
Glucose	100	(50g)

Lifestyle with diabetes

You don't suddenly become an expert at managing diabetes. But with practice, you'll learn how to tran- sition from completing it to accepting it. See whether any of these suggestions are well-known or worth- while to attempt.

Do you recall when you first discovered you developed diabetes and learned to take care of yourself? It is not an overnight process. However, you can take small steps to enhance your health every day.

Make and consume wholesome food:

Utilizing our recipes will not only help you delightfully manage your diabetes but also provide you with a pastime that you can enjoy with your loved ones. Making good dietary choices will help you on your path to managing diabetes by reducing your blood glucose levels and enhancing overall health.

Healthy Nutrition:

Spend time preparing meals. By waiting in the drive-through, you aren't saving any time.

Find inexpensive, simple-to-make recipes online. Many are so delicious you'll want to eat them straight from the pan.

Be active most of the time:

Exercise remains onwwe of the finest free strategies for treating diabetes, so try to get moving most days! Find regular opportunities to work up a sweat and minor activities like walking and climbing stairs that you may do throughout the day.

Join a pal for a workout. Because you won't desire to let them down, you'll be more motivated to persevere.

Managing Stress:

To calm down and unwind, try meditation or yoga. To get started, pick one of the several free movies available online.

Be active! You may relax by going for a stroll, and the effects might endure for hours. Call or arrange to meet up with someone who can relate.

Additionally, you should always:

- Regularly check your blood sugar.
- Even if you are feeling well, take your medications as directed.
- Manage the psychological effects of diabetes.
- Attend doctor visits.

Coping with Diabetes:

You can begin to feel wonderful today and tomorrow by properly caring for yourself and your diabetes. You are more prone to the following when your blood glucose is near normal:

- Have greater vigor
- Become less thirsty and fatigued
- need to urinate less frequently
- Better healing
- Have reduced bladder or skin problems

Things to Remember Everyday:

Your blood glucose may increase under stress. Find out how to manage your stress. Try relaxing like breathing exercises, gardening, walking, meditating, engaging in a craft, or hearing your favorite artist.

If you're feeling sad, get assistance. You could feel better if you talk to a mental health professional, ther- apy group, clergyperson, companion, or close relative who will attend to your worries.

Even when you feel well, take the medications you need for your diabetes and other health issues. To avoid a sudden cardiac arrest, inquire with your doctor about the need for aspirin. Tell your doctor if you experience any adverse effects or cannot pay for your medications.

Examine your legs daily for edema, redness, blisters, wounds, and skin irritation. Any scars that do not heal should be reported to your medical staff.

To maintain the good health of your mouth, gums, and teeth, ensure that you brush and floss daily. Give up smoking. To quit, get assistance.

Monitor your blood glucose levels. Try to check it several times per day. Make sure to discuss it with your medical staff. If your doctor recommends it, monitor your blood pressure and document it.

30 DAY MEAL PLAN

	BREAKFAST	SNACKS	LUNCH	DINNER	DESSERTS
DAY 1	Banana Pancakes	Multi-Seed Crackers	Spinach & Mushroom Quiche	Creamy spinach chicken	Shortbread Cookies
DAY 2	Breakfast Tacos	Almost Chipotle's Guacamole	Herby Fish with Wilted Greens & Mushrooms	Smoked salmon layer	Pumpkin Pie Spices Cookies
DAY 3	Crustless Quiche Lorraine	Cucumber Sandwich	Cauliflower Hash with Sausage & Eggs	Chicken breast with avocado salad	Coconut Flour Cookies
DAY 4	Lower Carb Strawberry Smoothie	Avocado Hummus	Bacon & Broccoli Egg Burrito	Flattened chicken with tomatoes, olives & capers	Shredded Coconut Cookies
DAY 5	Coconut & Spinach Smoothie	Deviled Eggs	Cheddar & Kale Quiche	Fish with peas & lettuce	Lemon Cookies Sweets
DAY 6	Mediterranean Salad	Black Bean Dip	Nutty chicken satay strips	Baked Stuffed Fish For One	Keto Chocolate Cake
DAY 7	Walnut and Cilantro Salad	Spiced Crackers	Chinese Turkey curry	Tuna Salad	Low Carb Vanilla Cake
DAY 8	Avocado Keto Toast Recipe	Sweet Potato Chips	Ginger & soy salmon en papillote	Healthy Chicken Salad with Greek Yogurt	Cream Cheese Pound Cake
DAY 9	Easy Egg Salad	Tomato-Cheddar Cheese Toast	Greek Chicken Meal Prep Bowls	Baked Salmon & Leek parcel	Blueberry Dump Cake
DAY 10	Tomato Mushroom Omelet	Garlic Hummus	Cajun Shrimp and Sausage Vegetable	Tarragon, mushroom & sausage frittata	Diabetic Cheesecake

30 DAY MEAL PLAN

	BREAKFAST	SNACKS	LUNCH	DINNER	DESSERTS
DAY 11	Veggie Breakfast Wrap	Sweet Potato Skins with Guacamole	Bruschetta Chicken	Ginger & soy salmon en papillote	Chocolate Mug Cake
DAY 12	Shakshuka	Beet Chips	Zucchini & Tomato Ragù	One-pot chicken chasseur	Carrot Cake with Cream Cheese Frosting
DAY 13	Bagel Seasoning Toast	Jicama Sticks	Chicken and Snap Pea Stir Fry	Superhealthy salmon burgers	Vanilla Mug Cake
DAY 14	Oatmeal & Cottage Cheese Pancake	Cheesy Kale Chips	Sheet-Pan	Chicken and mushrooms	Almond Flour Fudgy Brownies
DAY 15	Breakfast Sausage Patties	Apricot-Ginger Energy Balls	Lemon Butter Veggies and Sausage	Ginger Turkey	Coconut Flour Brownies
DAY 16	Low-Carb Smoothie Bowl with Berries	Lemon-Parm Popcorn	Cacio e Pepe Cauliflower	Aubergine, tomato & Parmesan bake	Fudgy Keto Brownies
DAY 17	Tequila and Grapefruit Juice	Flourless Banana Chocolate Chip Mini Muffins	Paleo Egg Roll in a Bowl	Pan-fried venison with blackberry sauce	Sugar-Free Chocolate Brownies
DAY 18	Overnight Oatmeal with Milk	Chile-Lime Peanuts	Vegan Keto Coconut Curry	Spicy Island Shrimp	Oat Flour Brownies
DAY 19	Broccoli Cheese Muffins	Pea Pods with Honey-Mustard Dipping Sauce	Lemon Salmon with Garlic and Thyme	Shrimp and Spinach Salad with Hot Bacon	Sugar-free Coffee Chocolate Brownies
DAY 20	Almond milk with blueberries smoothie	Chewy Granola Bars	Caprese Sandwich Tomato Chicken Burgers with Avocado Basil Aioli	Easy oven-roasted broccoli	Protein Loaded Brownies

30 DAY MEAL PLAN

	BREAKFAST	SNACKS	LUNCH	DINNER	DESSERTS
DAY 21	Flourless Savory Cheddar Zucchini Muffins	Homemade Trail Mix	Chipotle Chicken Fajitas	Creamy Turkey mushrooms skillet	Tapioca and Almond Flour Scones
DAY 22	Healthy Turkey and Bacon Muffin	Keto Cheese Crackers	Salmon Salad with Avocado and Grape Tomatoes	Chicken, Spinach, Mushroom Casserole	Keto Blueberry Scones
DAY 23	Keto Egg Muffins	Eggplant Chips	High Taste Zoodles	Cabbage and Eggs	Oat and Coconut Flour Scones
DAY 24	Gluten-Free Parmesan Biscuits	Plantain Chips	Tofu Scramble	One Pan Egg and Turkey Skillet	Greek Yogurt Chocolate Fudge Pops
DAY 25	Spinach Mushroom Egg and Ham Cups	Chocolate Banana Pops	Mussels in red pesto	Ricotta, tomato & spinach frittata	Maple Pecan Scones
DAY 26	Sausage and Fresh Basil Fast Frittata	Seasoned Pumpkin Seeds	Lobster with Thermidor butter	Pistachio Crusted Salmon	Keto Eggless Scones
DAY 27	Low-Carb Granola Bars with Nuts and Seeds	Basil and Pesto Hummus	Thai Crab Omelet	Thai Peanut Chicken Curry	Apple-Sauce Cinnamon Scones
DAY 28	Cauliflower Hash with Sausage & Eggs	Caprese Skewers	Spaghetti Squash Bolognese	Garlic Butter Shrimp with Spinach and Feta	Creamy Butterscotch Ice Cream
DAY 29	Tomato-Parmesan Mini Quiches	Dry Fruit Bits	Halibut with Lemon, Spinach, and Tomatoes	Seared Tilapia With Spiralized Zucchini	Low Carb and Sugar Ice Cream
DAY 30	Parmesan Cloud Eggs	Crispy Chickpeas	Baked Cod with Vegetables	Turkey Tenderloin	Soft Vanilla Protein Ice Cream

BREAKFAST RECIPES

BANANA PANCAKES

Total Servings: 2
Difficulty: Easy
Preparation Time: 10 minutes
Cook Time: 0 minutes
Total Time: 10 minutes

Ingredients

- 2 medium eggs
- 1/2 medium banana
- 1 scoop protein powder

Directions

1. Use a blender to make the eggs and banana smooth. Lightly grease the large non-stick skillet and heat it over medium heat. For each pancake, use 2 tablespoons of batter. Cook for 3-4 mins or until bubbles appear on the surface and the edges look dry.
2. Flip the pancakes carefully with a thin spatula and cook for 1 to 2 more until the bottoms are browned. Put the pancakes on a plate. Again, lightly oil the pan and do it again with the rest of the batter.

Nutrition Information:
Calories: 149kcal, Carbohydrates: 8g, Protein: 16g, Fat: 5.4g

BREAKFAST TACOS

Total Servings: 2
Difficulty: Easy
Preparation Time: 5 minutes
Cook Time: 5 minutes
Total Time: 10 minutes

Ingredients

- Salt and pepper as per taste
- 1/8 tsp. chili powder
- 1/8 tsp. cumin
- 6 medium eggs
- ½ cup cottage cheese
- 2 whole wheat flour tortilla
- ¼ cup fresh tomato salsa
- ¼ avocado, sliced
- 2 tbsp, chopped cilantro

Directions

1. Scramble the eggs in a small bowl until they are all mixed. Put aside and add spices. Coat a medium-sized skillet with organic butter or non-stick oil spray and heat it over low to medium heat.
2. Once the pan is hot, add the eggs and scramble them slowly for about 5 to 7 minutes until they are done. Add cheese, do so when the eggs are almost done.
3. Put off the heat when the eggs are done all the way through and no longer runny. Divide the eggs between the tortillas, then add salsa, avocado, and cilantro. Enjoy!

Nutrition Information:
: Calories: 2600kcal, Carbohydrates: 8g, Protein: 21g, Fat: 16g

PARMESAN CLOUD EGGS

Total Servings: 4
Difficulty: Medium
Preparation Time: 15 minutes
Cook Time: 15 minutes
Total Time: 30 minutes

Ingredients

- 1 scallion, chopped
- ¼ cup finely grated Parmesan cheese
- 6 medium eggs, yolks, and whites separated
- salt as per taste
- Ground pepper as per taste

Directions

1. Set the oven temperature to 450°F. Wrap parchment paper around a large baking sheet. Spray a little cook- ing spray on it. Separate the egg parts and put each yolk in its small bowl. In a bowl, use an electric mixer on high speed to beat all the egg whites and salt until they are stiff.
2. With a rubber spatula, gently fold the Parmesan and scallions into the beaten whites. Make 4 mounds of the egg-and-cheese mixture on the baking sheet that has been set up. Produce a well in the middle of each mound.
3. Bake the egg whites for about 3 minutes or until they start to get a light brown color. Remove from oven. If the well has filled up during baking, use the spoon to make it again.
4. Put an egg yolk into each hole. Bake for 3 to 5 minutes or until the yolks are cooked but still runny. Put pep- per on it. Serve right away.

Nutrition Information:
Calories: 94kcal, Carbohydrates: 1.4g, Protein: 7.8g, Fat: 6.2g

CRUSTLESS QUICHE LORRAINE

Total Servings: 5
Difficulty: Easy
Preparation Time: 10 minutes
Cook Time: 20 minutes
Total Time: 30 minutes

Ingredients

- 1 cup grated Gruyere cheese
- 2/3 cup milk
- 1/4 cup half & half cream
- 2 tbsp. chopped chives
- pinch freshly grated nutmeg
- 6 medium eggs
- 1/2 tsp. kosher salt
- cooking spray
- 6 strips of center-cut bacon
- 1/8 tsp. ground black pepper

Directions

1. Set your oven's temperature to 350F. Spray oil on a pie dish. Preparing the bacon: Put a large pan on medi- um heat to heat up. Put a single layer of bacon strips on the bottom of the pan.
2. Slowly cook the bacon strips, turning them over every so often until they are nicely browned. Lay the stripes on the paper towel and cut the cooked bacon crosswise into ¼-inch to ½-inch pieces. Spread the bacon out evenly in the dish and sprinkle the grated gruyere cheese on top.
3. Mix the milk, half-and-half, eggs, salt, black pepper, and nutmeg in a bowl with a whisk. Pour the custard into the dish and sprinkle the top with chives. Bake for 35 minutes. The quiche should be cut into six pieces and served.

Nutrition Information:
: Calories: 205kcal, Carbohydrates: 2.5g, Protein: 16g, Fat: 14g

Total Servings: 2
Difficulty: Easy
Preparation Time: 5 minutes
Cook Time: 00 minutes
Total Time: 5 minutes

LOWER CARB STRAWBERRY SMOOTHIE

Ingredients

- 1 cup unsweetened almond milk
- ½ cup low-fat Greek-style yogurt
- 5 medium strawberries
- 6 ice cubes

Directions

1. Put all ingredients into the blender and process them until they are completely smooth. After it has been poured, garnish the glass with a strawberry.

Nutrition Information:
: Calories: 334kcal, Carbohydrates: 6.5g, Protein: 8g, Fat: 3g

Total Servings: 1
Difficulty: Easy
Preparation Time: 5 minutes
Cook Time: 00 minutes
Total Time: 5 minutes

COCONUT & SPINACH SMOOTHIE

Ingredients

- ¼ tbsp. coconut milk
- 1 cup spinach
- 1 scoop protein powder

Directions

1. Put all ingredients listed above into a blender until the mixture has a smoothie consistency. Devour it as soon as possible.

Nutrition Information:
: Calories: 135kcal, Carbohydrates: 5g, Protein: 23.1g, Fat: 2.9g

MEDITERRANEAN SALAD

Total Servings: 24
Difficulty: Easy
Preparation Time: 15 minutes
Cook Time: 00 minutes
Total Time: 15 minutes

Ingredients

- 1 medium tomato
- 1 large cucumber
- 2 small radishes
- 1/2 medium red onion
- 1 carrot, peeled
- 1/2 red pepper, cleaned
- 1 tbsp parsley
- 1 tbsp. mint leaves
- 1 lemon
- 1/4 cup extra virgin olive oil
- salt as per taste
- 1 pepper as per taste

Directions

1. Prepare the vegetables by chopping them very finely and combining them in a bowl.
2. After squeezing the juice of the lemon over the salad, add the olive oil, salt, and pepper to taste, then toss everything together and serve.

Nutrition Information:
Calories: 144kcal, Carbohydrates: 8.4g, Protein: 1.3g, Fat: 12.8g

WALNUT AND CILANTRO SALAD

Total Servings: 3
Difficulty: Easy
Preparation Time: 20 minutes
Cook Time: 00 minutes
Total Time: 20 minutes

Ingredients

Salad
- 2 cups of cilantro leaves, chopped
- 3 cups flat-leaf parsley, chopped
- 1 cup mint leaves, chopped
- 1 cup fresh walnuts

Dressing
- ¼ cup olive oil
- Juice of one lime
- Salt & pepper as per taste
-

Directions

1. Mix the cilantro, parsley, and mint leaves in a salad bowl. Put the walnuts in a plastic bag and use the handle of a knife or another blunt object to crush them. Make sure you only do a little.
2. Included in the salad. Mix the olive oil, lime juice, salt, and pepper in a shaker. Shake it up well, then pour it over the salad.

Nutrition Information:
Calories: 273kcal, Carbohydrates: 7g, Protein: 11.2g, Fat: 24.9g

Total Servings: 2
Difficulty: Easy
Preparation Time: 5 minutes
Cook Time: 7 minutes
Total Time: 12 minutes

AVOCADO KETO TOAST RECIPE

Ingredients

- salt as per taste
- ½ ripe avocado, chopped
- 1 slice of bread

Directions

1. 1.   Toast your bread until it turns golden brown and firm. Take the seed out of your avocado. Use a big spoon to get the avocado meat out. Put it in a bowl and use a fork to mash it until it's as smooth as you want.
2. 2.   Mix in a pinch of salt, and if you're going to, you can add more to taste on your toast, spread mashed avoca- do. Serve and enjoy.

Nutrition Information:
Calories: 230kcal, Carbohydrates: 5g, Protein: 8g, Fat: 21g

Total Servings: 3
Difficulty: Medium
Preparation Time: 5 minutes
Cook Time: 20 minutes
Total Time: 25 minutes

EASY EGG SALAD

Ingredients

- 1 tsp. Dijon Mustard
- 6 medium hard-boiled eggs
- 1/4 cup light mayonnaise
- 1/4 tsp. ground black pepper
- 1 stalks celery

Directions

1. Cut six hard-boiled eggs in half and remove three of the yolks. Add to the bowl and mash lightly with a fork.
2. Add the leftover ingredients and stir to mix them all. Toss well until all the ingredients are combined. Chill in the refrigerator for 20-25 mins (optional), then serve and enjoy.

Nutrition Information:
Calories: 140kcal, Carbohydrates: 4g, Protein:10g, Fat: 9g

TOMATO MUSHROOM OMELET

Total Servings: 4
Difficulty: Medium
Preparation Time: 10 minutes
Cook Time: 20 minutes
Total Time: 30 minutes

Ingredients

- 1½ cups white mushrooms, sliced
- 2 tbsp. feta cheese, lower fat
- 4 large eggs
- 1 cup cherry tomatoes, quartered
- 2 cups fresh chopped spinach
- 1/2 tsp seasoning, salt-free, extra-spicy
- 3 medium eggs, whites
- 1 cup onion, chopped
- 2 tsp. olive oil
- 1 tbsp. water

Directions

1. Put the large non-stick skillet over medium heat and heat the olive oil. Add the onion and cook for approxi- mately 3 minutes, frequently stirring, until soft. Add the mushrooms and cook for around 4 minutes, stirring frequently.
2. Cook the tomatoes until they have lost most of their moisture. Cook the spinach for an additional minute af- ter adding it. Combine the spicy seasoning, egg whites, eggs, and water with a whisk. Reduce the heat and add the eggs. Cook without stirring until it begins to set.
3. Then, turn the egg mixture using a spatula until it is nearly set. Remove the pan and allow the eggs to finish cooking in the residual heat. Garnish with feta. Cut the loaf into four wedges before serving.

Nutrition Information:
Calories: 140kcal, Carbohydrates: 7g, Protein: 12g, Fat: 8g

VEGGIE BREAKFAST WRAP

Total Servings: 2
Difficulty: Easy
Preparation Time: 10 minutes
Cook Time: 10 minutes
Total Time: 20 minutes

Ingredients

- 2 tbsp. salsa
- 1/2 cup egg white
- 1 cup sliced mushrooms
- 1 cup firmly packed spinach
- 2 tbsp. scallions, chopped
- 1 non-stick cooking spray
- 2 medium eggs
- 2 whole wheat, low-carb flour tortillas
- 2 tsp. olive oil

Directions

1. Put olive oil in the pan and turn the heat to medium. Add the mushrooms and cook for about 3 minutes, until the edges are browned. Set the mushrooms aside.
2. Mix eggs with egg whites or egg substitute in a medium-sized bowl, either with a mixer or by hand, until well mixed. Stir in the chopped scallions and shredded spinach. You could also add fresh or dried herbs like basil or parsley for more flavor.
3. Start heating a medium-sized or large non-stick pan over medium-low heat. Spray the pan with a lot of cooking spray. Pour the egg mix into the pan and keep stirring it with a spatula as it cooks. When the eggs are done the way you like, take them off the heat and mix in the mushrooms.
4. In the middle of each tortilla, put half of the egg mixture. Put 1 tablespoon of fresh salsa or another sauce of your choice on top of each one. If you want, add more toppings like slices of avocado, bell pepper, or tomato, and then roll it up to make a wrap.

Nutrition Information:
Calories: 320kcal, Carbohydrates: 10g, Protein: 15g, Fat: 8g

Total Servings: 3
Difficulty: Medium
Preparation Time: 10 minutes
Cook Time: 15 minutes
Total Time: 25 minutes

SHAKSHUKA

Ingredients

- 1/3 tbsp chopped onion
- 2 tbsp. chopped bell pepper
- 1/4 tsp. paprika
- 4 medium eggs
- 1/4 cup fresh spinach
- 1/2 can diced tomatoes
- 1/3 tsp garlic, minced
- 1/2 tbsp. tomato paste

Directions

1. In a small pan, heat the olive oil over medium heat. Put in the onions, bell pepper, garlic, and spinach. Cook until the spinach starts to wilt and the onions start to brown.
2. Put tomato chunks, tomato paste, and spices in the pan. You can mash bigger pieces of tomato with the back of the spoon. Put down the heat to a simmer and wait about 5 minutes for the tomato mixture to thick- en.
3. Crack eggs carefully on top of the tomato mixture. Cover the pan and simmer until the eggs are done. Add optional toppings: feta, kalamata olives, and parsley. Enjoy!

Nutrition Information:
Calories: 114kcal, Carbohydrates: 7.4g, Protein: 8.5g, Fat: 6.1g

Total Servings: 2
Difficulty: Easy
Preparation Time: 5 minutes
Cook Time: 00 minutes
Total Time: 5 minutes

BAGEL SEASONING TOAST

Ingredients

- 1 slice of whole-grain bread
- salt as per taste
- 2/3 tsp. everything bagel sea-soning
- 4 tbsp. avocado, mashed

Directions

1. Toast the whole-grain bread in the toaster or a frying pan. Spread the mashed avocado over the toasted bread with a butter knife. Sprinkle salt with everything bagel seasoning. Serve and enjoy

Nutrition Information:
Calories: 119kcal, Carbohydrates: 7.5g, Protein: 2.2g, Fat: 4.4g

OATMEAL & COTTAGE CHEESE PANCAKE

Total Servings: 3
Difficulty: Easy
Preparation Time: 5 minutes
Cook Time: 15 minutes
Total Time: 20 minutes

Ingredients

- 1 cup almond flour
- 1 cup cottage cheese
- 2 eggs
- ¼ cup coconut flour
- 1 tsp baking powder
- 1 tsp vanilla extract
- ¼ tsp salt

Directions

1. In the food blender, blend the almond flour, cottage cheese, eggs, coconut flour, baking powder, vanilla ex- tract, and salt until smooth. Heat a non-stick skillet or griddle over medium heat. Grease with cooking spray or butter.
2. Pour ¼ cup of batter onto the skillet or griddle for each pancake. Cook until the edges look set, about 2-3 minutes. Then flip; cook more for 1-2 minutes.
3. Repeat with the leftover batter. Serve warm with low-carb syrup or butter and enjoy.

Nutrition Information:
Calories: 119kcal, Carbohydrates: 7.5g, Protein: 2.2g, Fat: 4.4g

BREAKFAST SAUSAGE PATTIES

Total Servings: 2
Difficulty: Medium
Preparation Time: 8 minutes
Cook Time: 10 minutes
Total Time: 18 minutes

Ingredients

- 1/2 tsp. onion powder
- 1/4 tsp. black pepper
- 1 tbsp. fresh parsley, chopped
- 1 tsp. poultry seasoning
- 1 tbsp. maple syrup
- 1 tsp. fennel seeds
- 2 lb. lean ground turkey
- 1/2 tsp. salt

Directions

1. Mix all ingredients thoroughly in a large bowl. Form the mixture into twenty-eight 2-inch patties.
2. Over medium-low heat, cook the patties in a large skillet for three to five minutes per side or until the center is no longer pink. Serve without delay.

Nutrition Information:
Calories:100kcal, Carbohydrates: 1g, Protein: 12g, Fat: 4.5g

LOW-CARB SMOOTHIE BOWL WITH BERRIES

Ingredients

- 1/3 cup pea protein powder
- 1 tbsp. coconut oil
- 56g fresh strawberries
- 1/2 tsp. psyllium husk powder
- 1/2 cup unsweetened almond milk
- 3 cups crushed ice
- 5-10 drops liquid Stevia

Directions

1. Allow the ice cubes to sit in the blender for five minutes. You want them to melt so that the blender has trac- tion slightly.
2. Blend the remaining ingredients until smooth, creamy, and pale pink. Transfer to a bowl and garnish with toppings of your choosing.

Nutrition Information:
Calories:100kcal, Carbohydrates: 1g, Protein: 12g, Fat: 4.5g

TEQUILA AND GRAPEFRUIT JUICE

Ingredients

- 1 tsp. lime juice
- 240g grapefruit
- 2 cups ice
- 283g pineapple
- 118ml tequila
- 2 tbsp. granulated sugar
- 2 tbsp. rosemary

Directions

1. In a large pitcher, mix tequila, grapefruit juice, pineapple juice, lime juice, and granulated sugar until the sugar is completely dissolved.
2. To serve, pour the beverage into serving glasses. Add ice and rosemary garnish. Serve.

Nutrition Information:
Calories: 75kcal, Carbohydrates:10.5g, Protein: 1g, Fat: 0g

Total Servings: 3
Difficulty: Easy
Preparation Time: 5 minutes
Cook Time: 15 minutes
Total Time: 20 minutes

OVERNIGHT OATMEAL WITH MILK

Ingredients

- ⅓ cup pine nuts
- 2 cups rolled oats
- 1 tsp. lemon zest
- ½ tsp. vanilla extract
- 2 fresh apricots, chopped
- 2 cups of low-fat milk

Directions

1. Mix milk with oats, lemon zest, and vanilla extract in a large bowl. Cover and put in the fridge for 8 hours to overnight, until the oats have soaked up the milk. Mix agave nectar, apricots, and pine nuts into the oatmeal.

Nutrition Information:
Calories: 86kcal, Carbohydrates:11g, Protein: 3g, Fat: 2.5g

Total Servings: 12
Difficulty: Medium
Preparation Time: 10 minutes
Cook Time: 20 minutes
Total Time: 30 minutes

BROCCOLI CHEESE MUFFINS

Ingredients

- 1 ½ tsp. coarse salt
- 1 tsp. onion powder
- 1 tbsp. olive oil
- 1 tsp. garlic powder
- 10 medium eggs
- 1 tsp. ground black pepper
- ¼ cup fresh milk
- 1 small head of broccoli, chopped into bite-size florets
- 1 tsp. dried mustard powder
- 1 cup shredded cheddar cheese, divided

Directions

1. Preheat oven to 350 degrees. In a non-stick skillet, warm up the olive oil over medium heat. Add the broccoli and cook for another 4–5 minutes until it is soft.
2. Mix the eggs, milk, salt, onion powder, garlic powder, crushed black pepper, and mustard powder in a large bowl. Add the broccoli that has been sautéed and half of the cheddar cheese.
3. Spray a muffin tin with 12 cups of cooking spray. Spread the egg mixture out evenly in each cup.
4. Spread the rest of the cheddar cheese on top. Bake for 18-22 minutes, until eggs are set. Let the muffins cool before taking them out of the pan.

Nutrition Information:
Calories: 316kcal, Carbohydrates: 7g, Protein: 21g, Fat: 23g

ALMOND MILK WITH BLUEBERRIES SMOOTHIE

Total Servings: 3
Difficulty: Easy
Preparation Time: 10 minutes
Cook Time: 00 minutes
Total Time: 10 minutes

Ingredients

- ¼ cup fresh spinach
- 1 tbsp. ground almonds
- ¼ cup fresh blueberries
- ½ cup unsweetened almond milk
- 1 tbsp. grapeseed oil
- 1 tbsp. ground chia seeds
- 1 tbsp. ground flax seed
- ½ cup Greek yogurt

Directions

1. Blend the spinach, blueberries, grapeseed oil, yogurt, almond milk, chia seeds, flax seed, and almonds until the mixture is completely smooth.

Nutrition Information:
Calories: 102kcal, Carbohydrates:5.5g, Protein: 3g, Fat: 2.5g

FLOURLESS SAVORY CHEDDAR ZUCCHINI MUFFINS

Total Servings: 8
Difficulty: Medium
Preparation Time: 10 minutes
Cook Time: 25 minutes
Total Time: 35 minutes

Ingredients

- ¼ tsp. black pepper
- 1 cup shredded and squeezed zucchini
- ½ tsp. onion powder
- ½ tsp. garlic powder
- 1 cup + 1 tbsp. shredded cheddar cheese
- 1¼ cup almond flour
- 3 medium eggs
- ½ tsp. baking soda
- ¼ tsp. coarse salt

Directions

1. Turn oven on to 350°F. Use a blender to blend the flour, eggs, baking soda, and spices until they are smooth. Add the zucchini and 1 cup of cheese. Pulse until the zucchini is evenly mixed in, but not so much that it is puree.
2. There you see small bits of green in the batter. Spoon about 3/4 of the batter into a muffin tin that has been lined. Add the extra 1 tablespoon of cheese on top. Bake at 350°F for about 25 minutes.
3. When the muffins are cool enough to touch, then remove them from the pan, serve and enjoy.

Nutrition Information:
Calories: 196kcal, Carbs: 5g, Protein: 10g, Fat: 15g

HEALTHY TURKEY AND BACON MUFFIN

Total Servings: 12
Difficulty: Hard
Preparation Time: 20 minutes
Cook Time: 25 minutes
Total Time: 45 minutes

Ingredients

- ½ jalapeno pepper, finely chopped
- 1 clove garlic, minced
- ½ cup lean turkey sausage, fully cooked
- ⅓ cup red bell pepper, diced
- 1 ½ cups baby spinach
- 12 slices lean turkey bacon
- ⅔ cup yellow onion, diced
- 1 tsp. black pepper
- 340g egg whites
- 3 medium eggs
- 1 ½ teaspoon salt

Directions

1. Turn the oven on to 350 °F (175 °C). Spray some cooking spray on a muffin pan or 12 muffin forms. Wrap the turkey bacon slice around the inside of each muffin hole. Put a small amount of spinach in the bottom of each muffin mold.
2. Cut the onions, jalapeno, and garlic into small pieces. In a medium frying pan sprayed with cooking spray, cook chopped vegetables over medium heat until the onions are clear, which takes about 4-5 minutes.
3. Take the onion mixture off the heat and place it on top of the spinach in each of the 12 muffin cups. Dice the bell pepper and cut the sausage into small pieces that are easy to eat. Put the mixture into the muffin tins.
4. Mix the egg whites, whole eggs, salt, and pepper in a bowl. Mix everything with a whisk. Pour enough egg mixture into the muffin tins to cover the vegetables.
5. Bake on the middle rack for 25 minutes. Remove the cups from the muffin tins for 5 minutes after you take them out of the oven.

Nutrition Information:
Calories: 116kcal, Carbohydrates: 2g, Protein: 13g, Fat: 6g

KETO EGG MUFFINS

Total Servings: 3
Difficulty: Easy
Preparation Time: 10 minutes
Cook Time: 12 minutes
Total Time: 22 minutes

Ingredients

- 8 egg yolks
- 4 fresh cherry tomatoes
- 1 cup mixed greens
- ½ tsp. garlic salt
- ¼ cup red onion, chopped
- ⅓ cup cooked bacon, crumbled
- 1⅓ cup cheddar cheese, shredded
- 3 tbsp. unsweetened almond milk (optional)

Directions

1. Turn the oven temperature on and set it to 400°F (200°C). Separate the egg parts and put the yolks in a large mixing bowl, and save the other part for later use.
2. Wash the mixed greens, tomatoes, and onion, and cut them into small pieces. Mix the egg yolks with the milk. Put the bacon, cheese, unsweetened almond milk, and garlic salt in a bowl. Blend well. Oil the muffin tin or line it with paper cups.
3. Pour the egg mix evenly into the muffin, about ¼ cup plus 1 tablespoon. Put the muffin pan in the oven for about 12 minutes or until the edges are slightly browned and toasty.
4. When the egg muffins are done, remove them from the oven and immediately sprinkle the tops with the cheddar cheese you set aside. Let the food sit out for 2 minutes to cool down.

Nutrition Information:
Calories: 408kcal, Carbs: 5g, Protein: 25g, Fat: 31g

Total Servings: 12
Difficulty: Easy
Preparation Time: 10 minutes
Cook Time: 00 minutes
Total Time: 10 minutes

GLUTEN-FREE PARMESAN BISCUITS

Ingredients

- 1/3 cup skim milk
- 3 tbsp. margarine
- 2 tbsp. Parmesan, freshly grated
- 1 cup baking mix

Directions

1. Preheat oven to 375 degrees F. Spray cooking spray on a baking sheet. Mix baking mix and margarine in a medium bowl. Mix with a fork and your hands to make large crumbs. Mix the milk into the mixture with a fork.
2. Add Parmesan cheese and mix it with the other ingredients. For each biscuit, drop about 1 tablespoon of the dough mixture at a time onto the baking sheet. Bake for about 12 minutes or until the top is golden brown.

Nutrition Information:
Calories: 408kcal, Carbs: 5g, Protein: 25g, Fat: 31g

Total Servings: 8
Difficulty: Easy
Preparation Time: 5 minutes
Cook Time: 10 minutes
Total Time: 15 minutes

SPINACH MUSHROOM EGG AND HAM CUPS

Ingredients

- 8 slice lower sodium deli-style ham
- 1/2 cup white mushrooms, diced
- 1 non-stick cooking spray
- 1/3 cup reduced-fat shredded cheddar cheese
- 2 tsp. olive oil
- 1 cup baby spinach, chopped
- 5 medium eggs
- 1/8 tsp. fresh ground black pepper

Directions

1. Put the oven temperature to 350F. Spray cooking spray on a muffin tin. Put a slice of ham in the 8th muffin cup. Put the oil in a sauté pan and turn the heat to medium-high. Cook for 3 minutes after adding the mush- rooms.
2. Cook for another 3 minutes after adding the spinach. Put the veggies somewhere to cool down. Whisk the eggs, spinach, mushrooms, pepper, and cheese together in a medium bowl (optional). Carefully pour the egg mixture into the 8 muffin cups lined with ham until they are 2/3 full.
3. Bake the eggs for 20 to 22 minutes or until they are fully cooked. Give it 5 minutes to cool down. Use a fork to loosen the ham and egg cups by going around the edges. Take each cup out with a fork.

Nutrition Information:
Calories: 190kcal, Carbohydrates: 6g, Protein: 21g, Fat: 8g

Total Servings: 4
Difficulty: Easy
Preparation Time: 10 minutes
Cook Time: 5 minutes
Total Time: 15 minutes

SAUSAGE AND FRESH BASIL FAST FRITTATA

Ingredients

- 226g chicken
- 4 oz. sausage
- 1 cup tomatoes, diced
- 2 tbsp. mozzarella cheese, shredded
- ¼ cup fresh basil, chopped
- 1½ cup egg substitute
- ½ cup green onion, chopped
- 2 tsp. extra Virgin Olive Oil

Directions

1. Heat the oil in a large skillet that doesn't stick on medium heat. Add the sausage and cook for 3 minutes, stirring every so often or until it starts to brown.
2. Spread the egg substitute evenly over the link and cook for 1 minute. Do not stir. Then, lift gently to let the raw egg flow under. Take off the heat.
3. Spread the cheese, green onions, tomatoes, and basil evenly.

Nutrition Information:
Calories: 190kcal, Carbohydrates: 6g, Protein: 21g, Fat: 8g

Total Servings: 12
Difficulty: Easy
Preparation Time: 5 minutes
Cook Time: 5 minutes
Total Time: 10 minutes

LOW-CARB GRANOLA BARS WITH NUTS AND SEEDS

Ingredients

- 30g hemp seeds
- 3 tbsp. sugar-free syrup
- 60g butter
- 285g almonds
- 30g pumpkin seeds
- 50g erythritol powder
- 30g coconut flakes
- 10ml vanilla extract
- ½ tsp. salt

Directions

1. Cover a 20 x 20 cm baking dish with baking paper. Mix the almonds, pumpkin seeds, coconut shreds, and hemp seeds in a bowl. Heat the syrup, butter, erythritol powder, and salt together for a few minutes while stirring until the mixture is smooth.
2. Remove from the heat and briefly pulse in the vanilla extract. Mix the syrup and nut mixture in a bowl, and then pour the mixture into the baking dish. Use a spoon to press the mix.
3. Let it cool to room temperature, then use baking paper to lift it from the dish. Cut into strips with care.

Nutrition Information:
Calories: 220kcal, Carbohydrates: 6g, Protein: 7g, Fat: 20g

Total Servings: 4
Difficulty: Medium
Preparation Time: 10 minutes
Cook Time: 15 minutes
Total Time: 25 minutes

EASY CAULIFLOWER HASH WITH EGGS

Ingredients

- 226g turkey sausage
- 8 medium eggs
- 3 tbsp. water
- 454g cauliflower rice
- 1 medium onion, diced
- ¼ tsp. salt
- 4 tbsp. olive oil, divided
- ⅛ tsp. ground pepper
- 2 cloves garlic, minced

Directions

1. Heat 2 teaspoons of oil on medium heat in a large non-stick skillet. Add the onion and garlic and cook while stirring until the onion is clear. Add the sausage and cook, stirring, for 4 to 5 minutes or until the sausage is done. Put the mix on a plate.
2. Turn the heat to medium-high and spread the cauliflower rice evenly in the pan. Cook without stirring for 2-3 mins or until it turns golden brown. Then stir, add salt, pepper, and water, and stir again.
3. Cover and cook for 3 to 4 minutes or until the food is soft and golden. Stir the sausage mixture and heat for about 2 minutes or until everything is hot. Heat 1 teaspoon of oil on medium heat in a medium non-stick pan. Put 4 eggs in the pan and cook for about 3 minutes, until the whites are set, but the yolks are still runny.
4. Place on a plate and do the same thing with 1 teaspoon of oil and the other 4 eggs. Put two fried eggs on each of the four plates on top of the hash.

Nutrition Information:
Calories: 317kcal, Carbohydrates: 7.8g, Protein: 25.9g, Fat: 18.8g

Total Servings: 6
Difficulty: Hard
Preparation Time: 25 minutes
Cook Time: 25 minutes
Total Time: 50 minutes

TOMATO- PARMESAN MINI QUICHES

Ingredients

- ½ cup sliced green onions
- 1 ¼ cups seeded and chopped Roma tomatoes
- 6 medium eggs, lightly beaten
- 1 tbsp. snipped fresh basil, crushed
- ⅔ cup finely shredded Parmesan cheese
- non-stick cooking spray
- 12 4-inch round thin slices lower sodium cooked ham
- ¼ tsp. black pepper

Directions

1. Set oven temperature to 350 degrees F. Coat 12 muffin cups 2½-inches in diameter with cooking spray. Fill muffin cups that have been ready with ham. Give each cup some tomatoes, green onions, basil, and pepper. Add cheese on top.
2. Place eggs on top of the tomato mixture. Bake for 23-25 mins, or until puffed and a knife comes out clean. Cool for 5 minutes in the cups. Take out of the cups. You can put more green onions and fresh basil on top. Warm up the food.

Nutrition Information:
Calories: 159kcal, Carbohydrates: 5g, Protein: 15g, Fat: 8g

SNACKS RECIPES

Total Servings: 12
Difficulty: Hard
Preparation Time: 15 minutes
Cook Time: 40 minutes
Total Time: 55 minutes

MULTI-SEED CRACKERS

Directions

1. Prepare the brown rice as directed on the packet, cool under chill running water, and set aside. Also, pre- pare quinoa as directed on the packet and rinse under chill running water. Drain the brown rice and quinoa well.
2. Put racks in the top and bottom parts of the oven. Set the oven heat range to 350°F to preheat. Cut three pieces of parchment paper the size of a large baking sheet.
3. In a food processor, combine the rice, quinoa, sesame seeds, flaxseeds, sunflower seeds, tamari, water, salt, and pepper. Process until the ingredients are finely chopped and can form a ball. The dough will stick together.
4. Cut the dough in two. Put one dough between two sheets of parchment paper that have been prepared. As thinly as possible, roll out. Take off the top sheet of parchment and put the dough on a baking sheet with the parchment.
5. Repeat with the rest of the dough and the paper that has been prepared. Bake for 15 minutes. Change where the baking sheets are and bake for another 12 to 15 minutes or until the edges are dark brown and the cookies are crisp.
6. Remove from the oven and carefully break into rough crackers. If some crackers aren't crispy enough, put them back in the oven for 5 to 10 minutes.

Ingredients

- ½ cup brown rice
- ½ cup quinoa
- 4 tbsp. sesame seeds
- 4 tbsp. flaxseeds
- 4 tbsp. sunflower seeds
- 2 tbsp. reduced-sodium tamari
- 2 tbsp. water
- Salt and crushed black pepper

Nutrition Information:
Calories per 2 crackers: 106kcal, Protein: 4g, Carbohydrate: 9g, Fat: 6g

Total Servings: 8
Difficulty: Easy
Preparation Time: 15 minutes
Cook Time: 00 minutes
Total Time: 15 minutes

ALMOST CHIPOTLE'S GUACAMOLE

Directions

1. Use a fork to mash the avocados in a bowl of medium size. Stir together the jalapeno, onion, cilantro, lime juice, and garlic until everything is combined properly.

Ingredients

- 3 medium ripe avocados, halved and pitted
- 1 medium jalapeño pepper, chopped
- ¼ cup chopped red or white onion
- ¼ cup chopped cilantro
- 2 tbsp. lime juice
- ½ tbsp. minced garlic
- ½ tsp. salt

Nutrition Information:
Calories ¼ cup: 135kcal, Protein: 2g, Carbohydrate: 7g, Fat: 11g

CUCUMBER SANDWICH

Total Servings: 1
Difficulty: Easy
Preparation Time: 10 minutes
Cook Time: 00 minutes
Total Time: 10 minutes

Ingredients

- ¼ cup cream cheese
- 1 tbsp. low-fat plain Greek yogurt
- 1 tbsp. sliced fresh chives
- 1 tbsp. chopped fresh dill
- ¼ tsp. ground pepper
- 2 low-carb bread slices
- ⅓ cup sliced cucumber

Directions

1. Mix the cream cheese, yogurt, chives, dill, and pepper in a small bowl until they are well mixed. Spread the mixture on one side of each piece of bread in an even layer.
2. Slices of cucumber go on top of one slice of bread, and the other slice, cream cheese side down, goes on top. Cut the sandwich in half diagonally and remove the crusts.

Nutrition Information:
Calories: 342kcal, Protein: 19g, Carbohydrate: 8g, Fat: 26g

AVOCADO HUMMUS

Total Servings: 10
Difficulty: Easy
Preparation Time: 10 minutes
Cook Time: 00 minutes
Total Time: 10 minutes

Ingredients

- 420g canned chickpeas, without salt
- 1 ripe avocado, halved and pitted
- 1 cup fresh cilantro leaves
- 4 tbsp. tahini
- 4 tbsp. extra-virgin olive oil
- 4 tbsp. lemon juice
- ½ tbsp. minced garlic
- 1 tsp. ground cumin
- ½ tsp. salt

Directions

1. Drain the chickpeas but keep 2 tablespoons of the cooking liquid. Put the chickpeas and the liquid you set aside in a food processor. Add avocado, cilantro, tahini, oil, lemon juice, garlic, cumin, and salt.
2. Blend until smooth as silk. Serve with pita chips, vegetable chips, or raw vegetables.

Nutrition Information:
Calories per ¼ cup: 169kcal, Protein: 4g, Carbohydrate: 9g, Fat: 13g

DEVILED EGGS

Total Servings: 12
Difficulty: Easy
Preparation Time: 10 minutes
Cook Time: 00 minutes
Total Time: 10 minutes

Ingredients

- 12 large eggs
- ¼ cup nonfat plain Greek yogurt
- 4 tbsp. mayonnaise
- 1 tbsp. minced shallot
- 1 tbsp. dill relish
- 2 tsp. Dijon mustard
- 1 tsp. white-wine vinegar
- Salt and crushed black pepper
- Pinch of paprika powder

Directions

1. Put one layer of eggs in a pan and cover it with water. Over medium-high heat, bring to a boil. Turn the stove flame to low and cook for 10 minutes at a very low simmer.
2. Take the pot off the heat, pour hot water, and cover the eggs with water that is as cold as ice. Wait until it's cool enough to touch.
3. Use a sharp knife to peel the eggs and cut them in half down the middle. Take the yolks out carefully and put them in a food processor. Add yogurt, mayonnaise, shallot, relish, mustard, vinegar, salt, and pepper, and blend until smooth.
4. Fill each egg white half with about 1 tablespoon of the filling. Just before serving, sprinkle with paprika.

Nutrition Information:
Calories per egg: 50kcal, Protein: 6g, Carbohydrate: 2g, Fat: 2g

BLACK BEAN DIP

Total Servings: 4
Difficulty: Easy
Preparation Time: 5 minutes
Cook Time: 10 minutes
Total Time: 15 minutes

Ingredients

- 175g black beans, low-sodium, and rinsed
- ¼ cup low-fat Greek yogurt
- 2 tsp. lime juice
- ½ tsp. ground cumin
- ½ tsp. dried oregano
- ½ tsp. garlic powder
- ¼ tsp. smoked paprika powder
- Salt and crushed black pepper
- ¼ tsp. cayenne pepper
- 2 tsp. olive oil
- 4 tbsp. chopped cilantro
- 4 tbsp. chopped onion

Directions

1. In a food blender, combine the beans, yogurt, lime juice, cumin, oregano, garlic powder, paprika, salt, and pepper. About 20 seconds should be enough time to mix everything well.
2. Add cayenne to taste, up to ¼ tsp, to make the dip spicier. Add oil, onion, and cilantro. Pulse for about 20 seconds or until well mixed. Place the food in a bowl to serve.

Nutrition Information:
Calories per ¼ cup: 105kcal, Protein: 5g, Carbohydrate: 10g, Fat: 5g

SPICED CRACKERS

Total Servings: 8
Difficulty: Easy
Preparation Time: 5 minutes
Cook Time: 10 minutes
Total Time: 15 minutes

Ingredients

- 3 tbsp. extra-virgin olive oil
- ½ tbsp. paprika powder
- ½ tbsp. dried oregano
- Pinch of salt
- 3 cups whole-grain crackers

Directions

1. Set oven temperature to 300 degrees F. Mix the oil, paprika, oregano, and salt in a large bowl. Add the crackers or chips and toss to coat. Spread on a baking sheet with a rim. Bake for 10 minutes. Cool for 10 minutes on the pan.

Nutrition Information:
Calories per ¼ cup: 111kcal, Protein: 2g, Carbohydrate: 10g, Fat: 7g

SWEET POTATO CHIPS

Total Servings: 8
Difficulty: Medium
Preparation Time: 5 minutes
Cook Time: 60 minutes
Total Time: 1 hr 5 mins

Ingredients

- 1 medium sweet potato, sliced into thick rounds
- 1 tbsp. canola oil
- Salt and crushed black pepper

Directions

1. Put slices of sweet potato in a large bowl of chilled water and let them soak for 20 minutes. Drain and use paper towels to dry. Put the sweet potatoes back in the bowl that was left dry. Add oil, salt, and pepper, and toss gently to coat.
2. Spray cooking spray on the air fryer basket. Put in the basket just enough sweet potatoes to make a single layer. Cook at 350 degrees F for about 15 minutes, turning and rearranging into a single layer every 5 min- utes, until cooked and crispy.
3. Carefully take the chips out of the air fryer and put them on a plate using tongs. Do the same thing with the rest of the sweet potatoes. Wait 5 minutes for the chips to cool down, then serve immediately.

Nutrition Information:
Calories: 36kcal, Protein: 0.5g, Carbohydrate: 4g, Fat: 2g

Total Servings: 1
Difficulty: Easy
Preparation Time: 5 minutes
Cook Time: 00 minutes
Total Time: 5 minutes

TOMATO- CHEDDAR CHEESE TOAST

Ingredients

- 1 diagonal slice baguette (¼-inch thick), whole-wheat
- 2 small slices of tomato
- 1½ tbsp. shredded cheddar cheese
- Pinch of cracked black pepper

Directions

1. Toast the bread in the toaster or toast the slices in a pan or oven. Add some pepper, tomato, and cheese to the top. If you want the cheese to melt, you can do so in a toaster oven or under the broiler.

Nutrition Information:
Calories: 36kcal, Protein: 0.5g, Carbohydrate: 4g, Fat: 2g

Total Servings: 8
Difficulty: Easy
Preparation Time: 7 minutes
Cook Time: 00 minutes
Total Time: 7 minutes

GARLIC HUMMUS

Ingredients

- 420g canned chickpeas, without salt
- ¼ cup tahini
- 4 tbsp. extra-virgin olive oil
- 4 tbsp. lemon juice
- ½ tbsp. minced garlic
- 1 tsp. ground cumin
- ½ tsp. chili powder

Directions

1. Drain the chickpeas, making sure to save ¼ cup of the liquid. Put the chickpeas and the liquid you set aside in a food processor.
2. Add tahini, oil, lemon juice, garlic, cumin, chili powder, and salt. Pulse for 2 to 3 minutes until the mixture is very smooth.

Nutrition Information:
Calories: 164kcal, Protein: 4g, Carbohydrate: 10g, Fat: 12g

Total Servings: 8
Difficulty: Medium
Preparation Time: 15 minutes
Cook Time: 2 Hours
Total Time: 2 hr 15 mins

SWEET POTATO SKINS WITH GUACAMOLE

Ingredients

Potato Skins:
- 4 small, sweet potatoes
- 1 tbsp. extra-virgin olive oil
- ⅛ tsp. salt
- ½ cup shredded cheddar cheese

Guacamole & Toppings:
- 1 ripe avocado
- 1 tbsp. lime juice
- ½ tbsp. minced garlic
- Pinch of salt
- ¼ cup chopped tomato
- 2 tbsp. minced red onion

Directions

1. Turn oven temperature to 400F to preheat. Wrap sweet potatoes tightly in aluminum foil and put them on a baking sheet. Bake for 50 mins-1 hour or until the meat is very soft. Unwrap it carefully and set it aside to cool. Put parchment paper on a baking sheet.
2. Cut potatoes in half and remove the insides, leaving a ¼-inch border. Put the skin side of the sweet potato halves down on the baking sheet. Spray oil and sprinkle salt over the potato skin. Roast for 27-30 minutes, until browned and crisp.
3. Cut each potato skin in half. Place on the baking sheet with the skin side down. Sprinkle 1 tablespoon of cheddar on each. Return to the oven and bake for 8-10 mins or until the cheese melts.
4. Make the guacamole in the meantime: In a small bowl, mash the avocado. Stir in lime juice, garlic, and salt. You can put guacamole, tomato, onion, and cilantro on top of each sweet potato skin.

Nutrition Information:
Calories: 120kcal, Protein: 3g, Carbohydrate: 9g, Fat: 8g

Total Servings: 5
Difficulty: Medium
Preparation Time: 10 minutes
Cook Time: 3 Hours
Total Time: 3 hr 10 mins

BEET CHIPS

Ingredients

- 2 large beets, thinly sliced
- 1 tbsp. extra-virgin olive oil
- ½ tsp. salt

Directions

1. Set oven temperature to 200 degrees F. Put parchment paper on 2 large baking sheets. Mix oil and salt with the beet slices. Spread in a single layer on the ready baking sheets.
2. Bake on the upper and lower oven racks until crisp, about 3 hours. Halfway through, turn the top of the pan to the bottom and front to back. Before serving, let the pans cool for 30 minutes.

Nutrition Information:
Calories: 39kcal, Protein: 1g, Carbohydrate: 3g, Fat: 3g

JICAMA STICKS

Total Servings: 5
Difficulty: Easy
Preparation Time: 5 minutes
Cook Time: 3 Hours
Total Time: 3 hr 10 mins

Ingredients

- 1 large jicama
- 4 tbsp. lime juice
- 1 tbsp. crushed red pepper

Directions

1. Using a potato peeler, peel the jicama and cut it into fries-size sticks. Add lime juice with crushed red pep- per in a bowl and toss well to coat. Serve as finger food.

Nutrition Information:
Calories: 39kcal, Protein: 1g, Carbohydrate: 3g, Fat: 3g

CHEESY KALE CHIPS

Total Servings: 1
Difficulty: Easy
Preparation Time: 10 minutes
Cook Time: 15 minutes
Total Time: 25 minutes

Ingredients

- ½ bunch of kale, washed and dried
- 2 tbsp. grated Parmesan cheese
- 2 tbsp. grated cheddar cheese
- 1 tbsp. olive oil
- Salt and crushed pepper to taste

Directions

1. Preheat the oven to 350F. Remove the kale leaves from the thick stems and tear them into bite-sized pieces. Toss the kale with olive oil, salt, and pepper in a large bowl.
2. Spread the kale out in a single layer on a baking sheet. Sprinkle the grated Parmesan and cheddar cheese over the kale. Roast for 10-15 minutes or until the cheese melts completely.
3. Serve warm and enjoy!

Nutrition Information:
Calories: 317kcal, Protein: 15g, Carbohydrate: 8g, Fat: 25g

Total Servings: 32
Difficulty: Medium
Preparation Time: 25 minutes
Cook Time: 00 minutes
Total Time: 25 minutes

APRICOT-GINGER ENERGY BALLS

Ingredients

- salt as per taste
- 6 tbsp. tahini
- 3 tbsp. honey
- ¾ cup finely shredded unsweetened coconut
- ¾ cup rolled oats
- 1 ½ cups dried apricots
- ¾ tsp. ground ginger

Directions

1. Mix the apricots, oats, coconut, tahini, honey, ginger, and salt in a food processor. Pulse 10 to 20 times until the ingredients are finely chopped. Then, process for about 1 minute, scraping the sides as needed, until the mixture is crumbly but can be pressed together to form a ball.
2. Wet your hands and roll about 1 tablespoon of the mixture into a ball with your hands. Put in a container to store. Do it again with the rest of the mix.

Nutrition Information:
Calories: 57kcal, Carbohydrates: 7.8g, Protein: 1.1g, Fat: 2.1g

Total Servings: 2
Difficulty: Easy
Preparation Time: 10 minutes
Cook Time: 00 minutes
Total Time: 10 minutes

LEMON-PARM POPCORN

Ingredients

- 3 cups air-popped popcorn
- 1 tbsp. freshly grated Parmesan cheese
- ½ tsp. lemon pepper
- salt as per taste
- 2 tsp. extra-virgin olive oil

Directions

1. Mix the lemon pepper, salt, and oil in a small bowl. Drizzle it over the popcorn, then toss it to coat it evenly.
2. Sprinkle shredded parmesan cheese on top, and it should be served right away.

Nutrition Information:
Calories: 99kcal, Carbohydrates: 9.7g, Protein: 2.3g, Fat: 5.9g

Total Servings: 24
Difficulty: Easy
Preparation Time: 20 minutes
Cook Time: 30 minutes
Total Time: 50 minutes

FLOURLESS BANANA CHOCOLATE CHIP MINI MUFFINS

Ingredients

- 1 tsp. baking powder
- ¼ tsp. salt
- 2 medium eggs
- ½ cup mashed ripe banana
- ¼ tsp. baking soda
- 1 ½ cups rolled oats
- ½ cup mini chocolate chips
- ⅓ cup packed brown sugar
- 3 tbsp. canola oil
- 1 tsp. vanilla extract

Directions

1. Turn the temperature in the oven up to 350 degrees F. Spray some cooking spray into a mini muffin tin that has 24 cups. In a blender, give the oats a few pulses until they are finely ground.
2. After adding the baking powder, soda, and salt, pulse the food processor once or twice to combine the ingredients. After adding the eggs, banana, brown sugar, oil, and vanilla extract, puree the mixture until it is completely smooth.
3. Mix in chocolate chips while stirring. Fill the muffin cups that have been prepared. Bake 15-17 mins. After five minutes of cooling in the pan on a wire rack, turn the cake out onto the rack to finish cooling.

Nutrition Information:
Calories: 78kcal, Carbohydrates: 10g, Protein: 1.4g, Fat: 3.6g

Total Servings: 48
Difficulty: Hard
Preparation Time: 10 minutes
Cook Time: 50 minutes
Total Time: 1 hr

CHILE-LIME PEANUTS

Ingredients

- 6 tbsp. chili powder
- 1/2-1 tsp. cayenne pepper
- 6 cups unsalted cocktail peanuts
- 4 tsp. kosher salt
- 6 tbsp. lime juice

Directions

1. Set the racks in the top and bottom thirds of the oven and heat it to 250 degrees F. Mix lime juice, chili pow- der, salt, and cayenne in a large bowl. Add the peanuts and stir to coat.
2. Spread evenly on two large, rimmed baking sheets. Bake until dry, about 45 minutes, stirring every 15 min- utes. Let cool down all the way. Put it in a container that won't let air in.

Nutrition Information:
Calories: 78kcal, Carbohydrates: 10.9g, Protein: 1.4g, Fat: 3.6g

Total Servings: 32
Difficulty: Easy
Preparation Time: 10 minutes
Cook Time: 15 minutes
Total Time: 25 minutes

PEA PODS WITH HONEY-MUSTARD DIPPING SAUCE

Ingredients

- 1 tsp. honey
- 1 tbsp. nonfat milk
- ¼ cup reduced-fat sour cream
- 1 tbsp. Dijon mustard
- 3 cups fresh pea pods

Directions

1. Mix the sour cream, milk, mustard, and honey in a small bowl. Refrigerate until ready to serve, covered with foil or plastic wrap. In the meantime, boil a small amount of lightly salted.
2. Add pea pods to the saucepan and boil for 2-4 minutes until the pea pods are crisp-tender. Drain and allow to cool. If you want to, chill. Use honey-mustard sauce to go with it.

Nutrition Information:
Calories: 40kcal, Carbohydrates: 8g, Protein: 2g, Fat: 0g

Total Servings: 54
Difficulty: Medium
Preparation Time: 10 minutes
Cook Time: 15 minutes
Total Time: 25 minutes

CHEWY GRANOLA BARS

Ingredients

- 2 cups miniature semisweet chocolate chips
- 1 tsp. vanilla extract
- 1 cup all-purpose flour
- 1 tsp. baking soda
- ⅔ cup softened butter
- 4 ½ cups rolled oats
- ½ cup honey
- ⅓ cup packed brown sugar

Directions

1. Put your oven temperature to 325 degrees F. Grease one 9x13-inch pan with a little oil. Mix the oats, flour, baking soda, vanilla, butter or margarine, honey, and brown sugar in a large bowl. Stir in the 2 cups of choc-olate chips. Press the mixture lightly into the pan. Bake for 19-22 mins or until golden brown.
2. Remove and cool for 3-4 minutes, then cut into bars. Let the bars cool completely before taking them out or serving them.

Nutrition Information:
Calories: 75kcal, Carbohydrates: 10.5g, Protein: 1g, Fat: 3.5g

Total Servings: 10
Difficulty: Easy
Preparation Time: 10 minutes
Cook Time: 00 minutes
Total Time: 10 minutes

HOMEMADE TRAIL MIX

Ingredients

- ¼ cup unsalted dry-roasted peanuts
- ¼ cup dried cranberries
- ¼ cup chopped pitted dates
- ¼ cup whole-shelled almonds, unpeeled
- 56g dried apricots

Directions

1. In a medium bowl, combine almonds, peanuts, cranberries, dates, and apricots (or any other fruit).

Nutrition Information:
Calories: 66kcal, Carbohydrates: 7.4g, Protein: 1.9g, Fat: 3.1g

Total Servings: 25
Difficulty: Easy
Preparation Time: 10 minutes
Cook Time: 30 minutes
Total Time: 40 minutes

KETO CHEESE CRACKERS

Ingredients

- ¾ cup Parmesan cheese, grated
- ½ cup medium-fat mozzarella
- 1 medium egg
- 1 cup + 2 tbsp. almond flour
- ¼ tsp. sea salt
- 2 tbsp. fresh rosemary
- 1 tsp. onion powder
- ½ tsp. garlic powder
- 15g cream cheese

Directions

1. Put your oven temperature to 425°F (220°C). Cut 2 baking pieces of paper into about 18 inches x 13 inches pieces. Mix the cream cheese, Parmesan, mozzarella, and almond flour in a large bowl that can go in the microwave.
2. Cook the mixture in the microwave for 30 seconds, stirring between them until it has melted and become very soft. Take it out of the microwave and stir it until it is smooth. Add the egg, rosemary, garlic powder, onion powder, and salt from the sea. Mix well and make a rough ball with it.
3. Put the dough in the middle of a sheet of baking paper while it is still warm. Place the other sheet on top, and then roll out the dough until it is even to the sheet's edges. Remove the top baking paper and put the dough on a large baking sheet. Cut off any rough edges or dough that hangs over.
4. Cut the dough into 1-inch squares with a pie crust cutter. Add coarse sea salt if you want to. Bake the crack- ers for 25 minutes, checking on them at 20 minutes to ensure they aren't getting too dark. If they are getting too brown, put a piece of foil over them for the rest of the baking time.
5. Remove from oven and let cool on the baking tray for 10 minutes. With a spatula, move the crackers to a wire cooling rack so they can cool completely.

Nutrition Information:
Calories: 53kcal, Carbohydrates: 3g, Protein: 1g, Fat: 5g

Total Servings: 25
Difficulty: Hard
Preparation Time: 10 minutes
Cook Time: 30 minutes
Total Time: 40 minutes

EGGPLANT CHIPS

Ingredients

- olive oil spray
- 2 tsp. sea salt
- 1 medium eggplant

Directions

1. Turn the oven on to 350°F/180°C. Use the kitchen to get thin and uniform slices of the eggplant. They will only get crispy if they are thick enough.
2. Sprinkle them with sea salt and let them "sweat" for about 30 minutes to draw out water. Get some paper towels and soak up as much water as you can.
3. Spray a baking dish with cooking spray. You could also line the pan with foil or parchment paper and spray that to make cleanup easier since some gooey middles might stick.
4. Place the eggplant slices on the pan without overlapping them. Spray the tops lightly and sprinkle them with the spices you want. After 20 minutes, turn the slices over and bake for another 10–20 minutes or until the edges start to brown and curl.
5. They should get a little harder, but they may still feel soft. After a few minutes out of the oven, they will get very crisp.

Nutrition Information:
Calories: 33kcal, Carbohydrates: 8g, Protein: 1.5g, Fat: 0.5g

Total Servings: 25
Difficulty: Medium
Preparation Time: 10 minutes
Cook Time: 30 minutes
Total Time: 40 minutes

PLANTAIN CHIPS

Ingredients

- salt as per taste
- 1 green plantain
- avocado oil spray

Directions

1. Set an air fryer to 350 degrees F and turn it on (175 degrees C). Remove both ends of the plantain; make slits along the side, only cutting through the skin. Peel the plantain's skin and cut it in half. Use a vegetable peeler to cut the peel into strips.
2. Spray avocado oil on the basket of the air fryer. Put strips of plantain in the basket, ensuring they don't touch each other. Oil the top of the plantain strips.
3. Cook for 7–9 minutes in an air fryer that has already been heated. Turn each strip over with tongs and cook for 3-5 mins or until it is crispy. Sprinkle salt on it right away.

Nutrition Information:
Calories: 25kcal, Carbohydrates: 7.5g, Protein: 0g, Fat: 0g

Total Servings: 25
Difficulty: Easy
Preparation Time: 15 minutes
Cook Time: 10 minutes
Total Time: 25 minutes

CHOCOLATE BANANA POPS

Ingredients

- 4 bananas, halved
- 42g unsweetened dark chocolate

Directions

1. Stick lollipop sticks into bananas, put them on the baking sheet, and freeze for an hour. Set the top of a dou- ble boiler over a pot of simmering water.
2. Until the chocolate is melted, which should take about 5 minutes, stir it often and use a non-stick spatula to scrape down the sides. Chocolate should be poured over frozen bananas.

Nutrition Information:
Calories: 25kcal, Carbohydrates: 7.5g, Protein: 0g, Fat: 0g

SEASONED PUMPKIN SEEDS

Total Servings: 16
Difficulty: Hard
Preparation Time: 20 minutes
Cook Time: 30 minutes
Total Time: 50 minutes

Ingredients

- 1 tbsp. olive oil
- 1 tbsp. chili powder
- 1 tbsp. tamari sauce
- 2 tsp. garlic powder
- salt as per taste
- 1-pound green hulled pumpkin seeds

Directions

1. Set oven temperature to 300 degrees F. (150 degrees C). In a 1-gallon bag that can be closed again, mix pumpkin seeds, olive oil, chili powder, tamari, and garlic powder.
2. Close the bag and knead the seeds to coat them with the spices. Spread the seasoned seeds evenly on a baking sheet. After 15 minutes in an oven that has already been heated, turn the seeds over.
3. Bake for about 15 more minutes or until the pumpkin seeds are lightly toasted and have a nice smell. Take it out of the oven and sprinkle a little salt on it. Cool before serving and store in the fridge in an airtight container.

Nutrition Information:
Calories: 164kcal, Carbohydrates: 6g, Protein: 7g, Fat: 14g

BASIL AND PESTO HUMMUS

Total Servings: 16
Difficulty: Easy
Preparation Time: 20 minutes
Cook Time: 30 minutes
Total Time: 50 minutes

Ingredients

- 1 clove garlic
- 1 tbsp. olive oil
- ½ tsp. balsamic vinegar
- ½ cup basil leaves
- 453g garbanzo beans, drained and rinsed
- ½ tsp. soy sauce
- salt and ground black pepper as per taste

Directions

1. In a food blender, pulse the garbanzo beans, basil, and garlic a few times. Use a spatula to push the mixture away from the bowl's sides. Mix the ingredients again as you drizzle in the olive oil.
2. Add the vinegar and soy sauce and pulse until they are mixed. Add salt and pepper to taste.

Nutrition Information:
Calories: 164kcal, Carbohydrates: 6g, Protein: 7g, Fat: 14g

Total Servings: 1
Difficulty: Easy
Preparation Time: 10 minutes
Cook Time: 00 minutes
Total Time: 10 minutes

CAPRESE SKEWERS

Ingredients

- 2 fresh and small low-fat cottage cheese balls
- 2 cherry tomatoes
- 3 fresh basil leaves
- Salt & ground pepper to taste

Directions

1. Thread cottage cheese, basil, and cherry tomatoes on small skewers as your desired patron.
2. Sprinkle salt and pepper and serve immediately.

Nutrition Information:
Calories: 54cal, Fat: 3g, Protein: 3g, Carb: 3g

Total Servings: 4
Difficulty: Easy
Preparation Time: 10 minutes
Cook Time: 00 minutes
Total Time: 10 minutes

DRY FRUIT BITS

Ingredients

- 10g chopped almonds
- 15g dried figs
- 19g dried apricots
- 2 tbsp. shredded coconut, unsweetened

Directions

1. Add almonds, figs, and apricots to a food blender; process until finely chopped.
2. Take out a small mixture, shape them into small balls, then dredge in coconut. Serve and enjoy.

Nutrition Information:
Calories: 68kcal, Fat: 4g, Protein: 2g, Carb: 6g

Total Servings: 2
Difficulty: Easy
Preparation Time: 6 minutes
Cook Time: 14 minutes
Total Time: 20 minutes

CRISPY CHICKPEAS

Ingredients

- ¼ cup canned unsalted chickpeas, rinsed, drained, and pat dried
- 1 tsp. toasted sesame oil
- Pinch of smoked paprika
- Pinch of crushed red pepper
- Pinch of salt
- 1 tsp. lime juice

Directions

1. Add chickpeas and oil with paprika, crushed red pepper, and salt to taste in a bowl. Coat the fryer basket with cooking spray.
2. Cook, shaking the basket occasionally, at 400 degrees F until very well browned, 12 to 14 minutes. Serve with lime wedges squeezed over the chickpeas.

Nutrition Information:
Calories: 132kcal, Fat: 3g, Protein: 3g, Carb: 6g

LUNCH RECIPES

Total Servings: 6
Difficulty: Medium
Preparation Time: 25 minutes
Cook Time: 40 minutes
Total Time: 1 hr 5 mins

SPINACH & MUSHROOM QUICHE

Ingredients

- 2 tbsp extra-virgin olive oil
- 8 oz. sliced fresh mixed wild mushrooms such as cremini, shiitake
- 1 ½ cups thinly sliced sweet onion
- 1 tbsp thinly sliced garlic
- 5 oz. fresh chopped baby spinach coarsely
- 6 large eggs
- ¼ cup whole milk
- ¼ cup half-and-half
- 1 tbsp Dijon mustard
- 1 tbsp fresh thyme leaves, extra for garnish
- ¼ tsp salt
- ¼ tsp ground pepper
- 1 ½ cups shredded Gruyère cheese

Directions

1. Preheat oven to 375F. Coat a pan with cooking spray; set aside. Heat oil in a large stainless steel skillet over medium-high heat; swirl to coat the pan. Add mushrooms; cook, occasionally stirring, until browned and tender, about 8 mins. Add onion and garlic; cook, often stirring, until softened and tender, about 5 mins. Add spinach; cook, constantly tossing, until wilted, 1-2 mins. Remove from heat.
2. Whisk eggs, milk, half-and-half, mustard, thyme, salt, and pepper in a medium bowl. Fold in the mushroom mixture and cheese. Spoon into the prepared pie pan. Then Bake until set and golden brown, about 30 mins. Let stand for 10 mins; slice. Garnish with thyme and serve.

Nutrition Information:
Calories: 277kcal, Protein: 17.1g, Carbohydrates: 6.5g, Fats: 20gg

---

Total Servings: 6
Difficulty: Medium
Preparation Time: 10 minutes
Cook Time: 20 minutes
Total Time: 30 minutes

HERBY FISH WITH WILTED GREENS & MUSHROOMS

Ingredients

- 3 tbsp olive oil, divided
- ½ sliced large sweet onion, sliced
- 3 cups sliced cremini mushrooms
- 2 sliced cloves garlic
- 4 cups chopped kale
- 1 diced medium tomato
- 2 tsp Mediterranean Herb Mix, divided
- 1 tbsp lemon juice
- ½ tsp salt, divided
- ½ tsp ground pepper, divided
- 4 (4 oz) cod, sole, or tilapia fillets
- Chopped fresh parsley for garnish

Directions

1. In a large saucepan, heat 1 tbsp of oil over medium heat. Add onion; cook, occasionally stirring, for 3-4 mins or until transparent. Add mushrooms and garlic; simmer, stirring periodically, for four to 6 mins or until the mushrooms release their liquid and begin to brown. Add kale, tomato, and a tsp of herb mixture. Cook for 5-7 mins, occasionally stirring, or until the kale is wilted and the mushrooms are soft. Add lemon juice and a pinch of salt and pepper. Remove from heat and keep warm while covered.
2. The fish should be seasoned with the remaining 1 tsp of the herb mixture and 1/4 tsp of salt and pepper. Heat the remaining 2 tbsp of oil over medium-high heat in a large stainless steel skillet. Add the fish and cook for 2-4 mins per side, depending on thickness, until the flesh is opaque. Transfer the fish to four plates or a dish for serving. Place vegetables on top of and around the fish; garnish with parsley, if desired.

Nutrition Information:
Calories: 214kcal, Protein: 18g, Carbohydrates: 11g, Fats: 11g

CAULIFLOWER HASH WITH SAUSAGE & EGGS

Total Servings: 4
Difficulty: Easy
Preparation Time: 10 minutes
Cook Time: 25 minutes
Total Time: 35 minutes

Ingredients

- 4 tsp olive oil, divided
- 1 diced small onion
- 2 minced cloves garlic
- 8 oz. turkey sausage
- 16 oz. cauliflower rice
- ¼ tsp salt
- ⅛ tsp ground pepper
- 3 tbsp water
- 8 large eggs

Directions

1. In a large stainless steel skillet, heat 2 tsp of oil. Add the onion and garlic, and cook while stirring until the onion is clear. Add the sausage and cook, stirring, for 4-5 mins or until the sausage is done. Put the mixture on a plate.
2. Turn the heat up to medium-high and spread the cauliflower rice out in a single layer in the pan. Cook with- out stirring for 2-3 mins or until it turns golden brown. Then stir, add salt, pepper, and water, and stir again. Cover and cook for 3-4 mins, or until the food is soft and golden. Stir the sausage mixture back in and let it heat up for about 2 mins.
3. Heat 1 tsp of oil on medium heat in a medium nonstick pan. Put 4 eggs in the pan and cook for about 3 mins, until the whites are set but the yolks are still runny (or up to 5 mins for firmer yolks). Place on a plate and do the same with the other 1 tsp of oil and the other 4 eggs. Put two fried eggs on each of the four plates on top of the hash.

Nutrition Information:
Calories: 317kcal, Protein: 26g, Carbohydrates: 7.8g, Fats: 18g

BACON & BROCCOLI EGG BURRITO

Total Servings: 1
Difficulty: Easy
Preparation Time: 10 minutes
Cook Time: 15 minutes
Total Time: 25 minutes

Ingredients

- 1 slice bacon
- 1 cup chopped broccoli
- ¼ cup chopped tomato
- 1 large egg
- 1 tbsp reduced-fat milk
- 1 scallion, sliced
- ⅛ tsp salt
- ⅛ tsp ground pepper
- 1 tsp avocado oil
- 2 tbsp shredded sharp Cheddar cheese

Directions

1. Cook the bacon in a medium stainless steel skillet over medium heat for 4-6 mins, rotating once or twice, until crisp. Transfer to a plate lined with paper towels. Add broccoli to the pan and stir-fry for 3 mins or until tender. Stir in the tomato, and then place in a small bowl.
2. In the meantime, combine egg, milk, scallion, salt, and pepper in a separate bowl. When the vegetables are finished cooking, clean the skillet. Add the vegetable oil and heat over medium heat. Add the egg mixture, turning the pan to coat the bottom. Cook, undisturbed, for approximately 2 mins or until the bottom is set.
3. Flip the egg "tortilla" with care using a thin, wide silicone spatula. Continue cooking until the cheese has completely melted, approximately 1 min longer. Place onto a plate. Fill the "tortilla" bottom half with the broccoli mixture, followed by the bacon. Roll carefully into a "burrito."

Nutrition Information:
Calories: 259kcal, Protein: 15g, Carbohydrates: 9g, Fats: 17g

Total Servings: 4
Difficulty: Medium
Preparation Time: 15 minutes
Cook Time: 50 minutes
Total Time: 1 hr 5 mins

Ingredients

- 2 tbsp sliced extra-virgin olive oil
- 2 large sliced shallots
- 1 (8-oz) bunch of lacinato kale, stemmed and roughly chopped
- 4 medium cloves garlic, chopped
- 1 tbsp cider vinegar
- 6 large eggs
- ¾ cup half-and-half
- ½ tsp salt
- ⅛ tsp ground nutmeg
- ¾ cup shredded extra-sharp yellow Cheddar cheese
- ¾ cup shredded aged sharp white Cheddar cheese

Total Servings: 2
Difficulty: Easy
Preparation Time: 10 minutes
Cook Time: 10 minutes
Total Time: 20 minutes

Ingredients

- 2 tbsp chunky peanut butter (without sugar)
- 1 grated garlic clove
- 1 tsp Madras curry powder
- few shakes of soy sauce
- 2 tsp lime juice
- 2 (300g) skinless chicken breast fillets cut into thick strips
- 1 cucumber, cut into fingers
- Sweet chili sauce to serve

CHEDDAR & KALE QUICHE

Directions

1. Turn oven on to 375°F. Cooking sprays a 9-inch deep-dish pie pan. Heat the oil in a large stainless steel skil- let over medium heat. Add the shallots and cook, stirring now and then, for 8-10 mins, until they are soft and starting to turn golden brown.
2. Add the kale and garlic and cook, folding and stirring the mixture all the time, for 5-8 mins, until the kale has wilted and is crisp-tender. Add vinegar, and then turn off the heat. All but 1/3 cup of the kale mixture should go into the pie pan. Set it aside for about 10 mins to cool down a bit.
3. In the meantime, break the eggs in a medium bowl and whisk them until they are smooth.
4. Add half-and-half, salt, and nutmeg with a whisk. Then sprinkle half of the yellow and half of the white Cheddar over the kale in the pie pan. Pour the egg mixture on top of the cheeses, and then add the rest of the cheeses on top.
5. Spread the 1/3 cup of kale you saved on top of the quiche. 35-40 mins, until golden brown, puffed around the edges, and set in the middle with a slight, firm jiggle. Let cool for about 10 mins before cutting and serving.

Nutrition Information:
: Calories: 301kcal, Protein: 15g, Carbohydrates: 9g, Fats: 23g

NUTTY CHICKEN SATAY STRIPS

Directions

1. Set the oven to 392F, and put nonstick paper on a baking tray.
2. In a bowl, combine 2 tbsp of chunky peanut butter, 1 finely grated clove of garlic, 1 tsp of Madras curry pow- der, a few shakes of soy sauce, and 2 tbsp of lime juice.
3. Add two chicken breast fillets without skin that has been cut into strips and mix well. Set on the baking sheet and bake for 8-10 mins, until cooked but still juicy.
4. Serve warm with about 10 cm of finger-sized cucumber and sweet chili sauce. You could also let it cool down and store it in the fridge for up to two days.

Nutrition Information:
: Calories: 276kcal, Protein: 41g, Carbohydrates: 3g, Fats: 10g

CHINESE TURKEY CURRY

Total Servings: 4
Difficulty: Easy
Preparation Time: 15 minutes
Cook Time: 40 minutes
Total Time: 55 minutes

Ingredients

- 4 skinless Turkey breasts, cut into chunks
- 2 tsp cornflour
- 1 diced onion
- 2 tbsp rapeseed oil
- 1crushed garlic clove
- 2 tsp curry powder
- 1 tsp turmeric
- ½ tsp ground ginger
- pinch sugar
- 400ml chicken stock
- 1 tsp soy sauce
- handful frozen peas
- rice to serve

Directions

1. Coat the turkey in cornflour and season thoroughly. Put it away. In a wok over low to medium heat, soften the onion for 5-6 mins in half of the oil before adding the garlic and cooking for one minute. Then, add the stock and soy sauce to a simmer and cook for 20 mins. Mix all ingredients in a food processor until smooth.
2. Clean the pan and cook the turkey in the remaining oil until it is golden brown on all sides. Tip the sauce to the pan, bring everything to a simmer, toss the peas and cook for 5 mins. If you wish to thin the sauce, add a small amount of water. Prepare with rice.

Nutrition Information:
: Calories: 264kcal, Protein: 40g, Carbohydrates: 7g, Fats: 8g

GINGER & SOY SALMON EN PAPILLOTE

Total Servings: 2
Difficulty: Medium
Preparation Time: 15 minutes
Cook Time: 25 minutes
Total Time: 40 minutes

Ingredients

- 2 tbsp light soy sauce
- 1 tbsp rice wine vinegar
- a thumb-sized piece of ginger, grated
- 1 grated garlic clove
- 2 skinless salmon fillets
- 1 courgette, spiralized into thin noodles
- 1 carrot, peeled, in spiralized into thin noodles
- 200g pak choi, leaves separated
- 1 sliced red chili
- Thai cauliflower rice to serve

Directions

1. Set the oven to 350F. Mix the soy sauce, vinegar, ginger, garlic, and some black pepper in a bowl before you cut up the vegetables. Add the salmon fillets, cover, and marinate for 10 mins at room temperature or up to 2 hours in the fridge.
2. Tear two pieces of baking paper big enough to wrap the fish and vegetables and put them on a baking tray. Place the vegetables in the middle of each piece of paper, and then put a bit of salmon that has been mar- inated and sliced chili on top of each one. Bring the sides of the parchment paper up over the salmon and pour half of the remaining marinade over each fillet. Then, scrunch the paper to seal the fish in a package.
3. Roast the salmon for 20–25 minutes until it is done, and flake it into large pieces. If you want, you can serve the fish in the package with cauliflower rice or regular rice.

Nutrition Information:
: Calories: 392kcal, Protein: 39g, Carbohydrates: 9g, Fats: 21g

Total Servings: 4
Difficulty: Hard
Preparation Time: 20 minutes
Cook Time: 20 minutes
Total Time: 40 minutes

GREEK CHICKEN MEAL PREP BOWLS

Ingredients

- 1 lb Chicken breast
- 1 ½ tsp Sea salt
- 3 tbsp Olive oil
- 1 tbsp Balsamic vinegar
- ½ tsp Black pepper
- 10 oz. Zucchini, sliced
- ½ lb Grape tomatoes (halved, ⅛1 cup)
- ½ large onion (cut into medium half moons, ⅓3/4 cup)
- ½ tbsp Dried dill
- ½ tbsp Dried parsley
- 1 tsp Dried oregano
- 1 tsp Garlic powder
- ¼ cup Feta cheese

Directions

1. Preheat oven to 400F. Prepare an extra-large baking sheet with foil and cooking spray. Fill a bowl with water. Stir with 2 tbsp of salt to dissolve. Add the chicken to the brine and sit for 10-20 mins.
2. Meanwhile, cut zucchini, grape tomatoes, and onions. In a small bowl, combine the dried herbs.
3. After the chicken is brined, pat it dry and set it in a single layer, close together but not touching, on a baking sheet.
4. Brush chicken with 1 tbsp olive oil. Season chicken with sea salt and black pepper. Sprinkle both sides with half the herb mixture.
5. Mix the chopped vegetables with the remaining 2 tbsp olive oil. Add sea salt, pepper, and herbs. Well-mix. Vegetables should not cover the chicken on the baking sheet.
6. If desired, drizzle balsamic vinegar over the chicken and vegetables. In the oven, roast the chicken and vegetables for about 20 mins, until the vegetables are tender and the chicken is cooked through. Take the saucepan out of the oven and rest for 5 mins. Transfer chicken slices to meal prep containers. Fill the plate with vegetables.

Nutrition Information:
Calories: 287kcal, Protein: 28g, Carbohydrates: 7g, Fats: 15g

---

Total Servings: 6
Difficulty: Easy
Preparation Time: 5 minutes
Cook Time: 10 minutes
Total Time: 15 minutes

CAJUN SHRIMP AND SAUSAGE VEGETABLE

Ingredients

- 1 lb large shrimp peeled and deveined
- 14 oz. sliced chicken sausage
- 2 sliced medium-sized zucchini
- 2 medium-sized yellow squash sliced
- ½ bunch of asparagus cut into thirds
- 2 red bell pepper chopped into chunks
- Salt and Pepper
- 2 tbsp olive oil
- 2 tbsp Cajun Seasoning

Directions

1. Put the shrimp, sausage, zucchini, yellow squash, asparagus, red bell pepper, salt, and pepper into a large bowl. Add olive oil and Cajun seasoning and toss until everything is covered.
2. Put in a large pan and turn the heat to medium-high. Cook for about 7 mins until the shrimp is pink and the vegetables are soft.
3. Garnish with fresh parsley if you want, and serve right away.

Nutrition Information:
Calories: 260kcal, Protein: 30g, Carbohydrates: 8g, Fats: 12g

Total Servings: 6
Difficulty: Easy
Preparation Time: 15 minutes
Cook Time: 15 minutes
Total Time: 30 minutes

BRUSCHETTA CHICKEN

Ingredients

- 4 boneless, skinless chicken breasts, thinly cut
- Kosher salt and black pepper to taste
- 2 tsp garlic powder
- 1 tbsp Italian seasoning
- 3 tbsp extra-virgin olive oil, divided
- 4 diced medium tomatoes
- ½ minced red onion
- 2 minced garlic cloves
- ⅛ cup fresh chopped fresh basil, plus more leaves for garnish
- Balsamic vinegar, for finishing
- Grated Parmesan cheese for finishing

Directions

1. Season the chicken on both sides with Kosher salt, pepper, garlic powder, and Italian seasoning.
2. Heat 2 tbsp of olive oil in a large skillet over medium heat. Put the chicken in the saucepan and cook well for 8-10 mins, until browned on both sides and fully cooked.
3. While the chicken is cooking, combine the remaining olive oil, tomatoes, red onion, garlic, and basil.
4. Distribute the tomato mixture on top of each chicken breast using a large scoop. Add more basil, balsamic vinegar, and Parmesan as garnishes. Serve without delay.

Nutrition Information:
Calories: 305kcal, Protein: 42g, Carbohydrates: 6g, Fats: 12g

---

Total Servings: 6
Difficulty: Easy
Preparation Time: 5 minutes
Cook Time: 10 minutes
Total Time: 15 minutes

ZUCCHINI & TOMATO RAGÙ

Ingredients

- 6 tbsp extra-virgin olive oil
- 1 onion, peeled and chopped
- 2 garlic cloves, peeled and crushed
- 1 sliced medium zucchini
- 1 sliced medium summer squash
- Kosher salt and freshly ground black pepper
- 7 oz. chopped ripe, flavorful tomatoes
- 4 oz. mozzarella, roughly torn
- ¼ cup chopped parsley leaves
- ¼ cup basil leaves, torn

Directions

1. Over medium heat, warm the oil in a stainless steel skillet. Add the onion and garlic and cook, often stirring, for 8-10 mins or until the onion is clear.
2. Salt and pepper to taste. Add the zucchini and summer squash. Cook, often stirring, for about 2 mins or until the zucchini and summer sauce is golden brown.
3. Stir in the tomatoes and cook for about 2 mins, or until the zucchini and summer squash is al dente and the tomatoes are just starting to soften. Serve with the cheese, parsley, and basil on top.

Nutrition Information:
Calories: 149kcal, Carbohydrates: 8g, Protein: 16g, Fat: 5.4g

Total Servings: 4
Difficulty: Easy
Preparation Time: 10 minutes
Cook Time: 10 minutes
Total Time: 20 minutes

CHICKEN AND SNAP PEA STIR FRY

Ingredients

- 2 tbsp vegetable oil
- 1 sliced bunch of scallions
- 2 minced garlic cloves
- 1 sliced red bell pepper
- 2½ cups snap peas
- 1¼ cups boneless skinless chicken breast, thinly sliced
- Salt and freshly ground black pepper
- 3 tbsp soy sauce or tamari
- 2 tbsp rice vinegar
- 2 tsp Sriracha (optional)
- 2 tbsp sesame seeds, more for serving
- 3 tbsp chopped fresh cilantro, more for serving

Directions

1. In a large saute pan, heat the oil. Add the scallions and garlic and cook for about 1 min or until the smell is nice. Add bell pepper and snap peas and cook for about 2-3 mins, until they are tender.
2. Add the chicken and cook for 4-5 mins, until the chicken is golden and fully cooked and the vegetables are soft.
3. Mix in the soy sauce, rice vinegar, sriracha (if using), and sesame seeds. Let the mixture cook for 1-2 mins on low heat.
4. Mix in the cilantro, then sprinkle sesame seeds and more cilantro. Serve right away.

Nutrition Information:
Calories: 228kcal, Protein: 20g, Carbohydrates: 11g, Fats: 11g

---

Total Servings: 6
Difficulty: Easy
Preparation Time: 15 minutes
Cook Time: 15 minutes
Total Time: 30 minutes

SHEET-PAN LEMON BUTTER VEGGIES AND SAUSAGE

Ingredients

- 4 tbsp unsalted butter, melted
- Zest and juice of 1 lemon
- 2 minced garlic cloves
- 4 medium carrots, peeled and diced
- 1 bunch of radishes, halved
- 2 diced red bell peppers
- 1 diced small eggplant
- Kosher salt and freshly ground black pepper
- 1 pint red cherry tomatoes
- 1 pint yellow cherry tomatoes
- 1 bunch asparagus
- 2 diced small zucchini
- 1½ pounds chicken sausage, sliced

Directions

1. Preheat the oven to 400F. In a bowl, stir together the butter, lemon zest, lemon juice, and garlic.
2. Arrange the carrots, radishes, bell pepper, and eggplant in an equal layers on a large baking sheet. Drizzle half of the lemon garlic butter over the vegetables and blend thoroughly. Salt and pepper are used as seasonings.
3. Roast for 15-17 mins or until the vegetables are barely soft. Add the sausage, tomatoes, asparagus, and zuc- chini. Drizzle the remaining lemon garlic butter over the mixture and mix thoroughly.
4. Roast for 17-20 mins, or until all the veggies are very soft and the sausage has begun to brown.

Nutrition Information:
Calories: 310kcal, Protein: 16g, Carbohydrates: 17g, Fats: 20g

Total Servings: 6
Difficulty: Easy
Preparation Time: 5 minutes
Cook Time: 10 minutes
Total Time: 15 minutes

CACIO E PEPE CAULIFLOWER

Ingredients

- 2 tbsp extra-virgin olive oil
- 4 tbsp unsalted butter, divided
- 1 head cauliflower, cut into bite-size florets
- 2 minced garlic cloves
- Kosher salt and freshly ground black pepper
- 2 tbsp all-purpose flour
- 1½ cups whole milk
- 2 cups grated Pecorino Romano

Directions

1. Olive oil and 1 tbsp of butter is heated over medium heat in a large skillet. Add the cauliflower and cook it for 8-9 mins, until it is soft. Add the garlic and toss until it smells good about 1 min. Add salt and pepper to taste.
2. Heat the last 3 tbsp of butter in a medium saucepan over medium heat. Add the flour and cook for 2 mins, stirring all the time.
3. Whisk the milk into the pot, then bring the whole thing to a simmer over medium heat. The sauce should get thicker as it cooks. Take the mixture off the heat and add the Pecorino while stirring. Use a lot more black pepper to season.
4. Mix the cauliflower into the sauce. Serve right away.

Nutrition Information:
Calories: 263kcal, Protein: 14g, Carbohydrates: 8g, Fats: 20g

Total Servings: 4
Difficulty: Easy
Preparation Time: 10 minutes
Cook Time: 10 minutes
Total Time: 20 minutes

PALEO EGG ROLL IN A BOWL

Ingredients

- 1½ tbsp sesame oil
- 3 carrots, peeled and shredded
- ¼ head red cabbage, shredded
- ¼ head green cabbage, shredded
- 1 bunch of scallions sliced on the bias
- 2 minced garlic cloves
- 1 tbsp minced ginger
- 1 pound ground pork
- 2 tbsp soy sauce or tamari
- 1½ tbsp unseasoned rice vinegar
- 1 tbsp sriracha
- Sesame seeds, cilantro leaves, and sliced red chiles for serving

Directions

1. Heat the oil in a medium-sized pan Over medium heat. Add the carrots, red cabbage, and green cabbage, and cook for about 3 mins, until the cabbage is soft.
2. Add garlic, ginger, and scallions and cook for about 1 min or until the mixture smells good. Add the pork and cook it for 6-7 mins, until it is fully cooked and no longer pink.
3. Soy sauce, rice vinegar, and sriracha are used to season the mix. Serve with red chiles, cilantro, and sesame seeds on top.

Nutrition Information:
Calories: 380kcal, Protein: 21g, Carbohydrates: 8g, Fats: 28g

Total Servings: 4
Difficulty: Easy
Preparation Time: 15 minutes
Cook Time: 15 minutes
Total Time: 30 minutes

VEGAN KETO COCONUT CURRY

Ingredients

- ¼ cup vegan butter
- ½ sliced green bell pepper
- 2 scallions, sliced, white and green parts kept separate
- 2 sliced garlic cloves
- 2½ tbsp vegan red curry paste
- 1 diced medium zucchini
- 1 diced medium carrot
- 1½ cups unsweetened full-fat coconut milk
- 1 cup vegetable stock
- 2 tbsp unflavored vegan protein powder
- 2 tbsp natural unsweetened peanut butter
- 4 drops liquid stevia
- 1 tsp sea salt
- Freshly ground black pepper
- 16 oz. extra-firm tofu, cut into medium dice
- 1 cup baby spinach
- ¼ cup chopped fresh cilantro, plus extra for serving
- 4 tbsp coconut oil, melted

Directions

1. Melt the butter in a big pot over medium heat. Add the bell pepper, scallion whites, and garlic; sauté for 1 min or until fragrant. Add the curry paste and simmer, constantly stirring, for approximately 1 min or until aromatic.
2. Stir in the zucchini, carrot, coconut milk, vegetable stock, protein powder, peanut butter, stevia, black pep- per, and salt. Lower heat to medium-low and simmer, uncovered, for 8-10 mins, or until the veggies are soft. If required, taste and adjust the seasoning.
3. Add the tofu and cook for 5 mins, stirring occasionally. Add the wilted spinach and cilantro. If required, taste and adjust the seasoning.
4. Distribute the curry across four bowls. Pour 1 tbsp of heated coconut oil onto each serving. Then add the scallion greens and more cilantro.

Nutrition Information:
Calories: 425kcal, Protein: 18g, Carbohydrates: 10g, Fats: 30g

---

Total Servings: 4
Difficulty: Easy
Preparation Time: 5 minutes
Cook Time: 20 minutes
Total Time: 25 minutes

LEMON SALMON WITH GARLIC AND THYME

Ingredients

- 4 5-6 oz salmon fillets
- Extra virgin olive oil, as needed
- Kosher salt and freshly ground black pepper
- 1 whole lemon, zested and sliced into thin rounds
- ½ tsp dried thyme
- 4-5 five garlic cloves, peeled and lightly crushed

Directions

1. Get the oven ready at 400°F.
2. Put the salmon fillets in an oven dish and drizzle olive oil. Then add salt and pepper, and sprinkle the lemon zest and thyme in an even layer. Set the lemon slices on top of the fillets and add the garlic cloves to the dish.
3. Put the salmon in the oven and bake for 18-20 mins, or until it is fully cooked and flakes apart with a fork.

Nutrition Information:
Calories: 356kcal, Protein: 32g, Carbohydrates: 3g, Fats: 23g

CAPRESE SANDWICH

Total Servings: 2
Difficulty: Easy
Preparation Time: 10 minutes
Cook Time: 00 minutes
Total Time: 10 minutes

Ingredients

- 4 slices of whole grain bread
- 4 slices of fresh mozzarella cheese
- 8 fresh basil leaves
- 8 slices of fresh tomato
- 2 tbsp balsamic glaze
- Salt and pepper, to taste

Directions

1. Toast the whole grain bread slices in a toaster. Assemble the sandwich by layering the mozzarella cheese, basil leaves, and tomato slices on one slice of the toasted bread.
2. Drop the balsamic glaze over the top of the sandwich. Add salt and pepper to taste. Place the other slice of toasted bread on top of the sandwich and press lightly to make it a sandwich.
3. Slice the sandwich in half and enjoy!

Nutrition Information:
Calories: 356kcal, Protein: 32g, Carbohydrates: 3g, Fats: 23g

TOMATO CHICKEN BURGERS WITH AVOCADO BASIL AIOLI

Total Servings: 4
Difficulty: Easy
Preparation Time: 10 minutes
Cook Time: 10 minutes
Total Time: 20 minutes

Ingredients

- Sun-Dried Tomato Chicken Burgers
- 1 lb ground lean chicken
- ¼ cup chopped sun-dried tomatoes
- 1 tsp garlic powder
- 1 tsp dried basil
- 1 tbsp coconut flour (optional)
- Salt and pepper, to taste
- Avocado Basil Aioli
- ½ cup mayo
- ½ small avocados (50 grams)
- 2 tbsp chopped packed basil
- 2 tbsp lemon juice
- Salt to taste

Directions

1. Start the grill and wait for it to get hot. Put all of the chicken burger ingredients into a medium bowl. If you use coconut flour, adjust it as needed. Mix well and shape into 4 patties of the same size. If you want to grill them, put them on a baking sheet and freeze them for 10 mins to make them firm. If you are pan-frying, there is no need to freeze.
2. Put the burgers on the grill directly over the heat and cook them for 4-5 mins per side, turning once.
3. Make the aioli while the burgers are cooking. Put everything into a large jar. Using an immersion blender, blend until smooth.
4. Serve burgers with aioli and your choice of toppings and sides. Enjoy!

Nutrition Information:
Calories: 240kcal, Protein: 24g, Carbohydrates: 4.6g, Fats: 14g

Total Servings: 4
Difficulty: Easy
Preparation Time: 10 minutes
Cook Time: 20 minutes
Total Time: 30 minutes

CHIPOTLE CHICKEN FAJITAS

Ingredients

- 1 lb chicken breasts, boneless and skinless, cut into thin strips
- 1 tsp ground cumin
- 1 tsp chili powder
- kosher salt
- pepper
- 1 tbsp canola oil
- 1 sliced red pepper
- 1 small sliced onion
- 1 cup sliced mushrooms
- 3 chopped cloves garlic
- 1 tbsp chopped chipotle chiles in adobo
- 1 ½ tbsp fresh lime juice

Directions

1. Cumin, chili powder, and 1/4 tsp each of salt and pepper are used to season the chicken. In a large cast-iron skillet, heat the oil over medium heat. Add chicken and simmer for 5-7 mins, stirring periodically, until cooked. Place on a platter.
2. Add red pepper, onion, mushrooms, and garlic to the same skillet and cook, turning periodically, until tender, 4-6 mins. Incorporate chipotle peppers, lime juice, chicken, and a bit of salt and pepper. Cook while stirring until thoroughly hot. Serve and Enjoy!

Nutrition Information:
Calories: 301kcal, Protein: 30g, Carbohydrates: 18g, Fats: 11g

SALMON SALAD WITH AVOCADO AND GRAPE TOMATOES

Total Servings: 4
Difficulty: Easy
Preparation Time: 5 minutes
Cook Time: 10 minutes
Total Time: 15 minutes

Ingredients

- 4 (4 oz) pieces of Wild Alaskan salmon fillet
- Kosher salt and black pepper
- 2 tbsp balsamic vinegar
- 2 tsp olive oil
- 1-pint grape tomatoes halved
- 2 scallions, thinly sliced
- ½ cup almond slivers, toasted
- 5 oz. mixed baby greens
- 1 sliced avocado

Directions

1. Turn oven on to 375°F. Salt and pepper the salmon with a half teaspoon of each, put it on a rimmed baking sheet and roast it for 10-15 mins, or until it is clear all the way through.
2. In the meantime, mix vinegar, oil, a pinch of salt and pepper, and a whisk in a large bowl. Add the tomatoes and stir them in. Mix in the scallions and almonds, and then toss the greens and avocado with the mixture. With salmon, serve.

Nutrition Information:
Calories: 340kcal, Protein: 37g, Carbohydrates: 11g, Fats: 22g Calories: 364kcal, Protein: 16g, Carbohydrates: 15g, Fats: 30g

Total Servings: 2
Difficulty: Easy
Preparation Time: 8 minutes
Cook Time: 7 minutes
Total Time: 15 minutes

HIGH TASTE ZOODLES

Ingredients

- 1 medium zucchini
- 1 cup fresh basil
- 1 tbsp pesto
- 1 handful of cherry tomatoes
- 1 handful walnuts
- Salt and pepper to taste

Directions

1. Use a spiral maker to make zoodles, which are noodles made from zucchini. If you don't have that magic thing, you can cut the zucchini into small pieces.
2. Into the pan, it goes with a little olive oil. Set the heat to medium. Cherry tomatoes should be cut in half and added to the pan. Add the nuts as well.
3. Throw it around. After about 7-8 mins, add the pesto and toss again. Basil leaves are used to finish off the zoodles. Ready. Enjoy!

Nutrition Information:
Calories: 149kcal, Carbohydrates: 8g, Protein: 16g, Fat: 5.4g

Total Servings: 2
Difficulty: Easy
Preparation Time: 5 minutes
Cook Time: 10 minutes
Total Time: 15 minutes

TOFU SCRAMBLE

Ingredients

- 1 tbsp olive oil
- 16 oz. block firm tofu
- 2 tbsp nutritional yeast
- ½ tsp salt, or more to taste
- ¼ tsp turmeric
- ¼ tsp garlic powder
- 2 tbsp non-dairy milk, unsweetened and unflavored

Directions

1. In a stainless steel pan, heat the olive oil over medium heat. Using a potato masher or fork, crush the block of tofu directly in the pan. You can also use your hands to crumble it into the pan. Stir constantly for 3-4 mins, until most of the tofu's moisture has evaporated.
2. Add nutritional yeast, salt, turmeric, and garlic powder now. Cook and stir continuously for approximately 5 mins.
3. Pour the dairy-free milk into the pan and swirl to combine. Serve immediately with bread, avocado slices, spicy sauce, parsley, steamed greens, and other breakfast dishes.

Nutrition Information:
Calories: 288kcal, Protein: 24g, Carbohydrates: 9g, Fats: 18g

Total Servings: 1
Difficulty: Easy
Preparation Time: 2 minutes
Cook Time: 10 minutes
Total Time: 12 minutes

MUSSELS IN RED PESTO

Ingredients

- 1 tsp olive oil
- 1 chopped shallot
- 1 small glass of white wine
- pinch crushed chili flakes
- 500g clean live mussels
- 2 tbsp red pesto
- crusty bread for serving

Directions

1. Heat the oil in a large stainless steel skillet and cook the shallots for 4-5 mins or until they are soft. Pour the wine in, sprinkle on the chili flakes, and let it bubble for 2 mins.
2. Pour in the mussels. Cover and cook for 5 mins or until all the shells have opened. Throw away any that are still closed. Add the red pesto and stir it in well. Pour into a large bowl and serve with crusty bread.

Nutrition Information:
Calories: 311kcal, Protein: 25g, Carbohydrates: 11g, Fats: 15g

Total Servings: 2
Difficulty: Medium
Preparation Time: 15 minutes
Cook Time: 15 minutes
Total Time: 30 minutes

LOBSTER WITH THERMIDOR BUTTER

Ingredients

- 2 cooked lobsters
For the butter
- 150ml dry white wine
- 1 chopped shallot
- a handful of tarragon leaves, chopped
- a handful of parsley leaves, chopped
- 1 tsp Dijon mustard
- ½ lemon juice
- pinch paprika
- dash Tabasco sauce
- 5 tbsp grated parmesan
- 140g butter, softened

Directions

1. Make the butter first. Mix the wine and shallot in a saucepan, then boil and simmer until nearly dry. Mix all the ingredients, roll into a log using cling wrap or aluminum foil, and then refrigerate until firm.
2. Remove the claws of the lobster. Using a big chef's knife, halve the lobster and rinse the head cavity with cold water before drying it with kitchen paper. e the lobsters on a baking sheet, and cut the side up. Remove the clawed flesh by fracturing the claws. Distribute crab claw meat among the cranial cavities.
3. Bring the grill to a high temperature. Thinly slice the butter and arrange it along the lobsters to cover all the meat. Grill for 5-8 mins, or until the butter begins to brown and bubble. Place the lobsters on plates and drizzle any remaining butter from the tray over the top. Serve alongside new potatoes and seasoned salad greens.

Nutrition Information:
Calories: 419kcal, Protein: 24g, Carbohydrates: 3g, Fats: 34g

THAI CRAB OMELET

Total Servings: 2
Difficulty: Easy
Preparation Time: 5 minutes
Cook Time: 10 minutes
Total Time: 15 minutes

Ingredients

For the Filling
- 5.3 oz can crab, drained
- 3 green onions, chopped
- 2 tbsp chopped cilantro leaves
- 1 tbsp ginger paste
- 1 tsp soy sauce
- 1 tsp lime juice
- ¼ tsp paprika
- salt and black pepper, to taste
- hot sauce, optional

For the Omelet
- 3 eggs
- 2 tbs canned unsweetened coconut milk
- black pepper
- nonstick spray

Directions

1. Combine the crab, green onions, cilantro, ginger paste, soy sauce, lime juice, and paprika to make the filling. Add salt and pepper to taste.
2. Mix the eggs, coconut milk, and black pepper lightly in a jug.
3. Spray a pan with something that won't make it stick, and then add the egg mixture. Once the bottom has set, carefully pull the edges toward the middle, letting the unset egg run underneath.
4. When the eggs are done, put the crab mixture in the middle of the omelet with a spoon.
5. Fold each side over, and let the crab warm up. Half it and serve.

Nutrition Information:
Calories: 190kcal, Protein: 20g, Carbohydrates: 4.6g, Fats: 9g

SPAGHETTI SQUASH BOLOGNESE

Total Servings: 5
Difficulty: Medium
Preparation Time: 25 minutes
Cook Time: 60 minutes
Total Time: 1 hr 25 minutes

Ingredients

- 4 tbsp olive oil
- 1 large spaghetti squash, halved crosswise and seeds removed
- Kosher salt and freshly ground black pepper
- 1 cup finely diced onion
- ½ cup finely diced carrot
- ½ cup finely diced celery
- 3 cloves garlic, minced
- 1 tbsp fresh thyme, chopped
- ½ tsp red pepper flakes
- 2 pounds of lean ground beef
- Two 24-ounce jars of good marinara sauce
- 1 cup grated Parmesan
- Chopped fresh basil for serving

Directions

1. Preheat oven to 400F. Using parchment paper, line a baking sheet.
2. Coat the inner side of the spaghetti squash with 2 tbsp of oil and a pinch of salt and pepper. Place cut-side down on the prepared baking sheet and bake for 40-45 mins or until fork-tender.
3. In the meantime, heat the remaining 2 tbsp of olive oil in a large skillet over medium heat. After heating the oil, add the onion, carrot, and celery. Season with a touch of salt and pepper, then simmer, occasionally turning, for about 5 mins or until the veggies are tender. Add the garlic, thyme, and red pepper flakes to the pan. Add the beef, crumbling it as you go, and heat for another 5 minutes or until fully browned. Stir in the marinara sauce to mix. Allow the sauce to boil for 15-20 mins or until the squash is cooked.
4. Remove the squash and allow it to cool for approximately 5 mins or until it is manageable. Utilizing a fork, separate the squash into spaghetti-like strands.
5. Serve the sauce over spaghetti squash noodles or within the squash halves, topped with Parmesan cheese and an abundance of basil.

Nutrition Information:
Calories: 270kcal, Protein: 15g, Carbohydrates: 11g, Fats: 19g

HALIBUT WITH LEMON, SPINACH, AND TOMATOES

Total Servings: 2
Difficulty: Easy
Preparation Time: 10 minutes
Cook Time: 10 minutes
Total Time: 20 minutes

Ingredients

- ¼ cup olive oil
- 2 6-oz halibut fillets
- Salt and freshly ground pepper
- 1 juiced lemon
- 1 tbsp butter
- 2 10-oz bags of baby spinach
- 3 crushed cloves garlic
- ½ tsp salt
- 6 diced Roma tomatoes
- ½ cup olive oil
- ½ cup chopped kalamata olives

Directions

1. As a garnish, fresh basil leaves. Put the olive oil in a large saute pan and heat it over medium-high heat. When the oil is hot, put the halibut steaks in the pan and cook for 3-4 mins on each side or until a fork can easily go into the fish. Add salt, pepper, and lemon juice to taste. Take it off the stove and keep it warm.
2. Heat the oil and butter over moderate heat in another large saute pan. Add the spinach slowly, along with the garlic that has been crushed and the salt. Saute the spinach until it is soft. Add lemon juice and pepper to taste.
3. Mix the tomatoes, olive oil, garlic, salt, and kalamata olives in a small saucepan. Fast heating over high heat keeps the tomatoes from turning into a sauce.
4. Place a piece of halibut in the middle of the spinach in the middle of each plate. Put the sauce on top of the halibut and add some fresh basil.

Nutrition Information:
Calories: 270kcal, Protein: 11g, Carbohydrates: 6g, Fats: 24g

BAKED COD WITH VEGETABLES

Total Servings: 6
Difficulty: Easy
Preparation Time: 15 minutes
Cook Time: 30 minutes
Total Time: 45 minutes

Ingredients

- 2 lb. cod fillets
- 5 small carrots
- 1 large onion
- 2 cups chopped celery
- 1 large bell pepper
- 16 oz. garlic pasta sauce
- 1 tbsp salt & pepper adjust to taste
- ½ tbsp ground black pepper
- 2 tbsp oil avocado

Directions

1. Dice all the veggies into tiny pieces. With a touch of avocado oil (1½ tbsp), sauté the vegetables in a big skillet. Stir the vegetables with the garlic pasta sauce to mix.
2. Place cod fillets on the bottom of a baking dish (grease with leftover oil). Sprinkle salt and crushed pepper on top. Spread the vegetable sauce on top of the fish.
3. Cover with a lid or aluminum foil. Bake at 350°F for 40 mins. Serve hot or cold, and relish!

Nutrition Information:
Calories: 223kcal, Protein: 29g, Carbohydrates: 13g, Fats: 6g

DINNER RECIPES

Total Servings: 4
Difficulty: Medium
Preparation Time: 10 minutes
Cook Time: 30 minutes
Total Time: 40 minutes

CREAMY SPINACH CHICKEN

Ingredients

- 1 oz. unsalted butter
- 8 1/2 oz baby spinach
- 4 chicken breasts, skin removed, sliced
- 4 chopped garlic cloves
- 200ml double cream
- 1.4 oz. Parmigiano Reggiano, grated
- cooked rice or potatoes, to serve (optional)

Directions

1. Melt half the butter in a large saucepan over medium heat. Add the spinach and cook it for about 2-3 mins until it starts to wilt. Mix well and add seasonings. Take out and put in a colander to drain.
2. If there is still liquid in the pan, pour it out and wipe it clean. Melt the rest of the butter in the same pan over medium heat by swirling it around so it covers the bottom. Fry the chicken for 1-2 mins, stirring it around until it turns golden. Prepare well. Then add garlic and cook for another min. Pour in the cream and let it simmer for 15 mins, often stirring, until the chicken is fully cooked. Be careful not to let the cream boil.
3. Stir in 30g of the cheese and all of the spinach, but first, squeeze out any extra water. Simmer for another 5 mins until the chicken is fully cooked and the cheese has melted. To see if the chicken is done, pierce the thickest part of the meat and make sure the juices run clear.
4. Sprinkle the remaining cheese on top, and serve the chicken with lots of sauce and rice or potatoes, if you like.

Nutrition Information:
Calories: 540kcal, Protein: 43g, Carbohydrates: 2g, Fats: 39g

Total Servings: 1
Difficulty: Easy
Preparation Time: 10 minutes
Cook Time: 10 minutes
Total Time: 20 minutes

CHICKEN BREAST WITH AVOCADO SALAD

Ingredients

- 1 chicken breast, skinless
- 1 tsp olive oil
- 1 heaped tsp smoked paprika
- ½ small diced avocado
- 1 tsp red wine vinegar
- 1 tbsp flat-leaf chopped parsley
- 1 medium chopped tomato
- half small sliced red onion

Directions

1. Warm up the grill to Medium. Rub 1 tsp of the olive oil and the paprika all over the chicken.
2. Cook for 4-5 mins on each side or until the meat has cooked. Mix the salad's ingredients, add salt and pep- per, and pour the rest of the oil on top.
3. Cut the chicken into thick pieces of slices and serve it with salad.

Nutrition Information:
Calories: 295kcal, Protein: 32g, Carbohydrates: 9g, Fats: 13g

Total Servings: 1
Difficulty: Easy
Preparation Time: 10 minutes
Cook Time: 10 minutes
Total Time: 20 minutes

FLATTENED CHICKEN WITH TOMATOES, OLIVES & CAPERS

Ingredients

- 1 boneless, skinless chicken breast
- A little seasoned flour for dusting
- 1 tbsp olive oil
- 1 large ripe chopped tomato
- 2 tsp capers
- handful olives
- Splash white wine
- Chopped chives

Directions

1. Open the chicken breast up like a book by cutting it almost in half. Flatten it with a rolling pin and lightly coat it with seasoned flour.
2. In a pan, heat the oil, add the chicken, and cook for 3–4 mins on each side until the chicken is crisp, browned, and cooked. Take it off the stove and keep it warm.
3. Add the tomato, capers, olives, and wine to the pan. Season to taste, then bring to a boil. For 2-3 mins, heat the sauce over low heat until the tomatoes start to break down. Pour it over the chicken and sprinkle with chopped herbs. With steamed potatoes, it tastes great.

Nutrition Information:
Calories: 335kcal, Protein: 36g, Carbohydrates: 9g, Fats: 15g

---

Total Servings: 1
Difficulty: Easy
Preparation Time: 5 minutes
Cook Time: 10 minutes
Total Time: 15 minutes

FISH WITH PEAS & LETTUCE

Ingredients

- 1 Little Gem shredded lettuce
- 2 spring thickly sliced onions
- handful frozen peas
- 1 tbsp olive oil
- 4.9 oz. boneless white fish fillet (tilapia)
- 1 tbsp reduced-fat crème fraîche

Directions

1. Combine lettuce, spring onions, and peas in a microwave-safe bowl. Drizzle the dish with olive oil.
2. Place fish fillet on the crème fraîche, then season. Cover with cling film and then puncture it.
3. Microwave for 6-8 mins on Medium until the tilapia is done. Remove fish from lettuce, then mix lettuce and peas thoroughly.
4. Place lettuce mixture and sauce on a platter, followed by the fish.

Nutrition Information:
Calories: 280kcal, Protein: 30g, Carbohydrates: 7g, Fats: 14g

Total Servings: 1
Difficulty: Easy
Preparation Time: 10 minutes
Cook Time: 30 minutes
Total Time: 40 minutes

BAKED STUFFED FISH FOR ONE

Ingredients

- 1 (8-ounce) catfish fillet
- pinch salt
- pinch coarsely ground black pepper
- 1 tsp olive oil
- 1 slice of diced bacon
- 2 tbsp diced celery
- 2 tbsp diced onions
- 1 minced garlic clove
- 1 tsp finely chopped parsley
- ½ tbsp salted butter, melted
- 2 tbsp white wine
- 2 tbsp grated Parmesan cheese
- pinch paprika

Directions

1. Heat the oven to 350F. Add salt and pepper to the fillet of fish. Set aside. Heat the oil on moderate heat in a skillet.
2. Sauté the bacon, celery, and onions until the bacon gets crispy, and the vegetables are tender.
3. Add the garlic and simmer for a further 2 mins. Stir in the parsley after removing the skillet from the heat.
4. Spread the mixture on the fish fillet, roll it, and secure it with a toothpick. Add a small amount of the melted butter to a small baking dish and swirl it to coat the bottom. Include fish. Pour the remaining butter over the fish, followed by the wine. Sprinkle with Parmesan cheese and paprika. Bake for 30 mins.

Nutrition Information:
Calories: 225kcal, Protein: 20g, Carbohydrates: 4g, Fats: 14g

Total Servings: 4
Difficulty: Medium
Preparation Time: 10 minutes
Cook Time: 10 minutes
Total Time: 20 minutes

TUNA SALAD

Ingredients

- 1 5-oz can water-packed tuna fish, drained
- 1 tbsp mayonnaise
- 1 stalk celery, diced
- 1 tsp olive oil
- ¼ tsp kosher salt
- ⅛ tsp coarsely ground black pepper
- ⅛ tsp garlic powder
- ½ tbsp pickle relish (optional)

Directions

1. With a fork, break up the tuna in a small bowl.
2. Mix the mayonnaise, celery, olive oil, salt, pepper, garlic powder, and relish. Taste it and add salt and pepper if you think it needs.
3. Serve immediately, or cover and put in the fridge until ready.

Nutrition Information:
Calories: 222kcal, Protein: 20g, Carbohydrates: 1g, Fats: 14g

Total Servings: 1
Difficulty: Easy
Preparation Time: 10 minutes
Cook Time: 10 minutes
Total Time: 20 minutes

HEALTHY CHICKEN SALAD WITH GREEK YOGURT

Ingredients

- 3 oz. cooked shredded chicken
- 2 tbsp plain nonfat Greek yogurt
- ¼ tbsp fresh parsley chopped finely
- 1/8 cup celery diced finely
- ¼ cup chopped apples
- 1 tbsp chopped pecans
- 1 tsp garlic powder
- 1 tsp pepper
- 1 tsp salt

Directions

1. Prepare chicken. Take a pot of water to a boil and boil the chicken for 10-14 mins. You can also use an Instant Pot, a crock pot, or buy a rotisserie chicken to cook chicken.
2. Chop the parsley, celery, apples, and pecans while the chicken is cooking. When the chicken is done cook- ing, use two forks to pull it apart and shred it.
3. Mix the chopped ingredients, spices, Greek yogurt, and shredded chicken in a bowl.
4. Mix everything with a spatula until all ingredients are well-covered in yogurt. Serve on a salad or a sand- wich.

Nutrition Information:
Calories: 184kcal, Protein: 23g, Carbohydrates: 7g, Fats: 7g

Total Servings: 2
Difficulty: Medium
Preparation Time: 10 minutes
Cook Time: 20 minutes
Total Time: 30 minutes

BAKED SALMON & LEEK PARCEL

Ingredients

- 8.8 oz. leek, sliced
- 85g mascarpone
- 1 tbsp chopped dill, plus 1 tsp
- 2 skinless salmon fillets
- ½ lemon, grated zest of 1/4, plus a good squeeze of juice
- 3 tsp capers
- spinach wilted, to serve (op- tional)

Directions

1. Adjust oven temperature to 392F. Place two sheets of baking paper large enough to wrap each salmon fillet in your work area.
2. Cover the leeks with 6 tbsp of water and boil in a saucepan. Cook for 5 mins or until the leeks are almost soft and the water has been absorbed. Mix in the mascarpone, 1 tbsp of dill, and seasonings.
3. Place half of the creamy leeks in the center of one sheet of parchment, followed by a salmon fillet, and continue with a second parcel. Sprinkle the lemon zest with lemon juice, then sprinkle the capers and the remaining 1 tsp dill.
4. Bring the parchment over the fish and attach the two edges by folding them over multiple times in the cen- ter.
5. Repeat with the ends and arrange the packages on a baking sheet with room between them.
6. Bake the bundle for 12-15 mins, then carefully open it. If desired, serve with lemon wedges for squeezing and wilted spinach.

Nutrition Information:
Calories: 480kcal, Protein: 32g, Carbohydrates: 4g, Fats: 36g

TARRAGON, MUSHROOM & SAUSAGE FRITTATA

Ingredients

- 1 tbsp olive oil
- 7 oz. sliced chestnut mushrooms
- 2 pork sausages
- 1 crushed garlic clove
- 3.5 fine asparagus
- 3 large eggs
- 2 tbsp half-fat soured cream
- 1 tbsp wholegrain mustard
- 1 tbsp chopped tarragon
- mixed rocket salad to serve

Directions

1. Turn up the heat on the grill. In a medium-sized, non-stick frying pan, heat the oil over high heat. Add the mushrooms and cook for 3 mins.
2. Make nuggets with the meat extracted from the skins of the sausages. Add them to the skillet and cook for a further 5 mins or until they are golden brown. Cook for another minute after adding the garlic and aspara- gus.
3. Whisk together the eggs, sour cream, mustard, and tarragon in a jug. Season the eggs well, and then pour them into the pan.
4. Cook for 3–4 mins, then place under the grill for another 1–2 mins, or until the top is set, but the middle is still a little loose. If you like, serve it with the salad leaves.

Nutrition Information:
Calories: 433kcal, Protein: 25g, Carbohydrates: 8g, Fats: 32g

GINGER & SOY SALMON EN PAPILLOTE

Ingredients

- 2 tbsp light soy sauce
- 1 tbsp rice wine vinegar
- ½ ginger, grated
- 1 garlic clove, grated
- 280g skinless salmon fillets
- 1 courgette, ends trimmed and spiralized into noodles
- 1 carrot and spiralized into noodles
- 2 bulbs of pak choi, leaves separated
- 1 red chili, sliced
- Thai cauliflower rice, to serve (optional)

Directions

1. Preheating the oven to 352F. Before preparing the vegetables, combine the soy sauce, vinegar, ginger, gar- lic, and black pepper in a bowl. Add the salmon fillets, cover, and marinate at room temperature for 10 mins or in the refrigerator for up to 2 hours.
2. Tear two pieces of baking parchment large enough to wrap the fish and veggies and place them on a baking sheet.
3. Place the vegetables in the center of each sheet of paper and top each with a salmon fillet marinated in soy sauce and sliced chili. Bring the sides of the parchment paper up over the salmon, pour half of the remaining marinade over each fillet, and then scrunch the parchment paper together tightly to seal the salmon.
4. Roast 20–25 mins until the fish is fully cooked and splits into large chunks. If desired, serve the fish in the bundle with cauliflower or ordinary rice.

Nutrition Information:
Calories: 391kcal, Protein: 39g, Carbohydrates: 9g, Fats: 21g

Total Servings: 1
Difficulty: Easy
Preparation Time: 10 minutes
Cook Time: 00 minutes
Total Time: 10 minutes

SMOKED SALMON LAYER

Ingredients

- ½ peeled carrot
- 2 trimmed radishes
- small chunk cucumber
- 3 tbsp full-fat soft cheese
- juice ½ lemon or lime
- a small handful of roughly chopped coriander leaves
- 2 slices smoked salmon
- drizzle of olive oil to serve (optional)
- bread and butter to serve

Directions

1. Grate the carrot, radishes, and cucumber, but throw away the seeds from the cucumber.
2. Mix in the cheese, lemon, or lime juice, and most of the coriander. Then add salt and pepper to taste.
3. Place one slice of salmon on a plate, top it with the vegetable mixture, and then drape the other slice over it. Sprinkle with the rest of the coriander, drizzle with olive oil, and serve with bread and butter.

Nutrition Information:
Calories: 231kcal, Protein: 16g, Carbohydrates: 6g, Fats: 15g

---

Total Servings: 4
Difficulty: Medium
Preparation Time: 20 minutes
Cook Time: 1 hr 30 mins
Total Time: 1 hr 50 mins

ONE-POT CHICKEN CHASSEUR

Ingredients

- 1 tsp olive oil
- 3.5g butter
- 4 chicken legs
- 1chopped onion
- 2 crushed garlic cloves
- 7 oz. pack small chestnut mushrooms
- 225ml red wine
- 2 tbsp tomato purée
- 2 thyme sprigs
- 500ml chicken stock

Directions

1. Heat 1 tsp of oil and half of the butter in a large lidded casserole.
2. Season 4 chicken legs, then fry them for about 5 mins on each side until they are golden brown. Take out and put away.
3. Melt the butter that is left in the pan. Add 1 chopped onion and cook for about 5 mins, until the onion is soft.
4. Add 2 cloves of crushed garlic and cook for about 1 min. Add 200g of a small button or chestnut mushrooms and cook for 2 minutes.
5. Stir in 2 tbsp of tomato purée, let the liquid bubble, and reduce for 5 mins, then add 2 thyme sprigs with 500ml of chicken stock and 225ml red wine.
6. Place the chicken legs back in the pan, cover, and cook on reduced heat for about an hour or until the chick- en is very tender.
7. Take the chicken legs out of the pan and put them somewhere warm. For about 10 mins, boil the sauce until it becomes syrupy and the flavor becomes concentrated.
8. Put the chicken legs back in the sauce and serve

Nutrition Information:
Calories: 439kcal, Protein: 35g, Carbohydrates: 7g, Fats: 28g

Total Servings: 4
Difficulty: Medium
Preparation Time: 20 minutes
Cook Time: 10 minutes
Total Time: 30 minutes

SUPERHEALTHY SALMON BURGERS

Ingredients

- 4 18 oz. boneless, skinless salmon fillets cut into chunks
- 2 tbsp Thai red curry paste
- thumb-size piece of fresh root ginger, grated
- 1 tsp soy sauce
- 1 bunch coriander, half chopped, half leaves picked
- 1 tsp vegetable oil
- lemon wedges to serve

For the salad:
- 2 carrots
- 1 small cucumber
- 2 tbsp white wine vinegar
- 1 tsp golden caster sugar

Directions

1. Put the salmon, paste, ginger, soy sauce, and chopped coriander in a food processor. Pulse until coarsely chopped.
2. Pour out the mixture and shape it into four patties. Heat the oil in a pan that won't stick, then fry the burgers for 4-5 mins on each side, turning them until they are golden brown.
3. In the meantime, use a swivel peeler to cut carrot and cucumber into thin strips and put them in a bowl. Toss with the vinegar and sugar until the sugar has dissolved, and then toss in the coriander leaves.
4. Split the salad among four plates. Serve with rice and burgers.

Nutrition Information:
Calories: 291kcal, Protein: 29g, Carbohydrates: 7g, Fats: 17g

---

Total Servings: 4
Difficulty: Easy
Preparation Time: 15 minutes
Cook Time: 25 minutes
Total Time: 40 minutes

CHICKEN AND MUSHROOMS

Ingredients

- 2 tbsp olive oil
- 17.6 oz. boneless, skinless chicken thigh
- flour for dusting
- 1.7 oz cubetti di pancetta
- 10.5 oz. small button mushroom
- 2 chopped large shallots
- 250ml chicken stock
- 1 tbsp white wine vinegar
- 1.7 oz. frozen pea
- A small handful of parsley, chopped

Directions

1. In a frying pan, heat 1 tbsp of oil. Season the chicken, dust it with flour, and then brown it on all sides. Re- move. Fry the pancetta and mushrooms until they are soft, then take them out.
2. Add the last tbsp of oil and cook the shallots for five mins. Then add the stock and vinegar and let them boil for 1-2 mins. Bring the chicken, pancetta, and mushrooms back to the pot and cook for 15 mins. Add the peas and parsley and continue cooking for 2 more mins.

Nutrition Information:
Calories: 260kcal, Protein: 32g, Carbohydrates: 3g, Fats: 13g

Total Servings: 6
Difficulty: Medium
Preparation Time: 20 minutes
Cook Time: 10 minutes
Total Time: 20 minutes

Ingredients

- 35 oz. pack boneless skinless chicken thighs
- 1/2 fresh ginger, peeled and chopped
- 4 garlic cloves, chopped
- 1 tsp mild chili powder
- 15g mass fresh coriander, chopped
- juice of 1 lime
- 2 tbsp sunflower oil
- 2 medium onions
- 1 tsp ground turmeric
- 400ml can reduced-fat coconut milk
- 1 fresh red chili, deseeded and sliced
- 1 chicken stock cube

Directions

1. Cut each chicken thigh into two or three large pieces and put them in a bowl with the ginger, garlic, chili powder, half coriander, lime juice, and 1 tbsp of oil. Mix well, cover, and put in the fridge until you're ready to cook. Do this in the morning or, even better, the night before for the best taste.

2. Peel and cut the onions into quarters, then use a food processor to chop them very finely. For a curry, you want the onions to be very small. In a large frying pan, heat the rest of the oil, add the onion, and stir-fry it for about 8 mins until it is soft. Add the turmeric, stir well, and cook for another min.

3. Pour the chicken and marinade mixture and cook over high heat until the chicken changes color. Pour in the coconut milk, add the chili and stock, cover, and let the chicken cook for 20 mins or until it's soft. Stir in the rest of the coriander, and then serve with pilau rice, mango chutney (we like Geeta's), and poppadoms or naan bread.

Nutrition Information:
Calories: 149kcal, Carbohydrates: 8g, Protein: 16g, Fat: 5.4g

Total Servings: 6
Difficulty: Medium
Preparation Time: 10 minutes
Cook Time: 50 minutes
Total Time: 60 minutes

AUBERGINE, TOMATO & PARMESAN BAKE

Ingredients

- 2 garlic cloves, crushed
- 6 tbsp olive oil
- 2 x 14 oz canned chopped tomatoes
- 2 tbsp tomato purée
- 4 aubergines, cut into long, thick slices
- 2.9 oz. parmesan, freshly grated
- 0.7 oz. pack basil leaves torn
- 1 egg, beaten

Directions

1. Adjust oven temperature to 392F. In a small dish, combine the garlic and 4 tbsp olive oil. Cook for 3 mins over high heat, then add the tomatoes and simmer for 8 mins, stirring occasionally. Incorporate the tomato purée.
2. Meanwhile, heat a griddle pan to a high temperature. Brush a few aubergines with a small amount of oil, then add them to the pan. Approximately 5-7 mins over high heat or until thoroughly browned and cooked. Halfway through cooking, flip them. Lift onto paper towels and continue with the next batch.
3. When the aubergines are cooked, place a couple in the bottom of an oven-safe dish and pour sauce over them. Sprinkle with Parmesan cheese and basil. Repeat this step with the remaining ingredients and sea- sonings. Pour the remaining egg over the top, sprinkle with additional Parmesan, and bake for 20 mins or until the topping is brown.

Nutrition Information:
Calories: 225kcal, Protein: 10g, Carbohydrates: 8g, Fats: 17g

Total Servings: 4
Difficulty: Easy
Preparation Time: 10 minutes
Cook Time: 15 minutes
Total Time: 25 minutes

PAN-FRIED VENISON WITH BLACKBERRY SAUCE

Ingredients

- 1 tbsp olive oil
- 2 thick venison steaks or 4 medallions
- 1 tbsp balsamic vinegar
- 150ml beef stock
- 2 tbsp redcurrant jelly
- 1 garlic clove, crushed
- 2.9 oz. fresh or frozen black-berry

Directions

1. In a saucepan, heat the oil and cook the venison for 5 mins, then flip it and cook for another 3-5 mins, depending on how rare you like the meat and how thick it is (cook for 5-6 mins on each side for well done). Remove the meat from the pan and put it somewhere else to rest.
2. Pour the stock, redcurrant jelly, and garlic into the pan. Then add the balsamic vinegar. Stir everything together while cooking over high heat; add the blackberries and keep cooking until they soften. Serve with deer meat, celeriac mash, and broccoli.

Nutrition Information:
Calories: 182kcal, Protein: 28g, Carbohydrates: 7g, Fats: 5g

SPICY ISLAND SHRIMP

Total Servings: 6
Difficulty: Easy
Preparation Time: 20 minutes
Cook Time: 20 minutes
Total Time: 40 minutes

Ingredients

- 1 large green pepper, chopped
- 1 chopped large onion
- 1/2 cup butter, cubed
- 2-1/4 lbs large uncooked shrimp, peeled and deveined
- 2 cans (8 oz each) of tomato sauce
- 3 tbsp chopped green onions
- 1 tbsp minced fresh parsley
- 1 tsp salt
- 1 tsp pepper
- 1 tsp paprika
- ½ tsp garlic powder
- ½ tsp dried oregano
- ½ tsp dried thyme
- ½ tsp white pepper
- ½ tsp cayenne pepper
- Optional: Hot cooked rice and thinly sliced green onions

Directions

1. Cook the green pepper and onion in butter in a large skillet until soft. Reduce the heat and add shrimp. Cook shrimp for 5 mins or until they turn pink.
2. Incorporate the tomato sauce, green onions, parsley, and seasonings into the mixture. Bring to a simmer. Re- duce heat; simmer, uncovered, for 20 mins or until the sauce has become thicker. Served with rice and more green onions, if preferred.

Nutrition Information:
Calories: 293kcal, Protein: 29g, Carbohydrates: 7g, Fats: 17g

SHRIMP AND SPINACH SALAD WITH HOT BACON

Total Servings: 6
Difficulty: Easy
Preparation Time: 20 minutes
Cook Time: 10 minutes
Total Time: 30 minutes

Ingredients

- 1-1/2 lb uncooked shrimp, peeled and deveined
- 1 tsp Montreal steak seasoning
- 4 chopped bacon strips
- 1 chopped shallot
- 1/3 cup cider vinegar
- 1 tbsp olive oil
- 1 tsp Dijon mustard
- ½ tsp sugar
- ½ tsp salt
- ¼ tsp pepper
- 1 package (10 oz) of fresh spinach
- ¾ cup julienned roasted sweet red peppers
- ¼ cup sliced almonds

Directions

1. Season shrimp with steak seasoning. On wooden skewers, thread shrimp. Grill shrimp, covered, over moder- ate heat or broil at a distance of 4 in. from the heat until pink, about 2-3 mins per side.
2. In the meantime, fry bacon in a large skillet over medium heat, tossing periodically until crisp. Using a slot- ted spoon, remove and drain on paper towels. Keep only 1 tbsp of drippings. Add shallot; cook and stir over medium heat for 1-2 mins or until tender. Add the next six ingredients and bring them to a boil. Turn off the heat.
3. In a large serving bowl, stir spinach with the dressing to coat. Shrimp and pepper slices are layered between bacon and almonds.

Nutrition Information:
Calories: 212kcal, Protein: 22g, Carbohydrates: 6g, Fats: 10g

Total Servings: 6
Difficulty: Easy
Preparation Time: 5 minutes
Cook Time: 10 minutes
Total Time: 15 minutes

EASY OVEN- ROASTED BROCCOLI

Ingredients

- 1 ½ lb broccoli, cut into florets
- 3 tbsp olive oil
- 3 minced cloves garlic
- sea salt and freshly gr black pepper, to taste

Directions

1. Set the oven temperature to 425F. Spray baking (large) sheet with non-stick spray.
2. Mix broccoli florets with olive oil, garlic, and salt&pepper to taste in a large mixing bowl. Add seasonings if you want to.
3. Put the broccoli in one layer on a baking sheet with a rim. For 18 to 20 mins, until the broccoli is soft and lightly browned. (Turn them over halfway through to cook them more evenly.)

Nutrition Information:
Calories: 110kcal, Protein: 3g, Carbohydrates: 8g, Fats: 8g

Total Servings: 3
Difficulty: Easy
Preparation Time: 5 minutes
Cook Time: 35 minutes
Total Time: 40 minutes

CREAMY TURKEY MUSHROOMS SKILLET

Ingredients

- 1 lb. turkey meat cut into bite-size pieces
- 4 oz. mushrooms quartered
- 1 cup bone broth
- 3 tbsp heavy cream
- 1 diced onion small
- 1 tsp garlic powder
- ½ tsp dried rosemary
- 2 tbsp butter
- sea salt and black pepper to taste

Directions

1. In a skillet, melt one tablespoon of butter over medium heat. Add turkey and simmer for 8-10 mins, until browned. Season with pepper and salt then set aside.
2. In a skillet, melt another tablespoon of butter over normal heat, then add diced onion and simmer for 3-5 mins or until softened. Add mushrooms and simmer for a further 8-10 mins.
3. Return the cooked turkey to the pan. Add garlic powder and rosemary, and simmer for an additional 10 mins. Add heavy cream and simmer for 1-2 mins.
4. If necessary, season with salt and pepper and serve immediately.

Nutrition Information:
Calories: 325kcal, Protein: 39g, Carbohydrates: 6g, Fats: 16g

CHICKEN, SPINACH, MUSHROOM CASSEROLE

Total Servings: 4
Difficulty: Medium
Preparation Time: 10 minutes
Cook Time: 40 minutes
Total Time: 50 minutes

Ingredients

- 2 cups chicken cooked, shredded
- 10 oz. button mushrooms sliced
- 6 oz. spinach, chopped
- ½ cup shredded mozzarella
- 2 tbsp chopped onion
- 1 tbsp butter
- 2 minced cloves garlic
- ½ tsp thyme
- ½ tsp red pepper flakes
- salt and pepper to taste
- For sauce
- ¾ cup heavy cream
- 3 oz. cream cheese
- 2 oz. mozzarella shredded
- ¼ cup Parmesan grated
- pinch nutmeg
- salt and pepper to taste

Directions

1. Turn the oven on to 350F.
2. In a pan over medium-high heat, melt the butter. Then add onion, garlic, and thyme. For 30 secs, cook. Add mushrooms and red pepper flakes, then season with salt and pepper and cook for 8 mins.
3. Stir in the spinach a handful one at a time, waiting for each handful to wilt before adding the next. Cook for another 2 mins or until the spinach wilts. Set aside.
4. Mix all of the sauce ingredients in a small saucepan. Heat on low and stir every so often until the cheese starts to melt and the sauce is creamy and uniform.
5. Put a layer of shredded chicken in the bottom of a casserole dish. Spread half of the cheese sauce on top, then put a layer of the mushroom-spinach mixture. Spread the rest of the sauce on top, sprinkle with mozza- rella, and bake for 20 mins until the top is golden brown and bubbly.
6. Let stand for 5 mins before serving and enjoy.

Nutrition Information:
Calories: 450kcal, Protein: 19g, Carbohydrates: 8g, Fats: 38g

CABBAGE AND EGGS

Total Servings: 2
Difficulty: Easy
Preparation Time: 5 minutes
Cook Time: 10 minutes
Total Time: 15 minutes

Ingredients

- 2 tbsp butter
- 2 minced garlic clove
- 2 cups lightly packed cabbage, shredded
- 4 eggs lightly beaten
- salt and pepper to taste

Directions

1. Cook food in a non-stick saucepan over medium heat.
2. Spread the butter throughout the pan.
3. Add the garlic and let it get aromatic for around 20 secs.
4. Add the cabbage and simmer, constantly stirring, for 3-5 mins, until it has softened. I prefer to heat mine until it begins to caramelize, which can take an additional min or two.
5. Distribute the cabbage in a thin layer.
6. Pour the eggs into the saucepan and tilt it slightly to spread them out.
7. Allow the eggs to cook for around 15-20 seconds, then gently fold them until they are fully done.
8. Immediately remove from heat and serve!

Nutrition Information:
Calories: 450kcal, Protein: 19g, Carbohydrates: 8g, Fats: 38g

Total Servings: 6
Difficulty: Easy
Preparation Time: 5 minutes
Cook Time: 20 minutes
Total Time: 25 minutes

ONE PAN EGG AND TURKEY SKILLET

Ingredients

- 1 lb ground turkey
- 1 cup salsa
- 6 eggs
- Salt and pepper to taste

Directions

1. Add ground turkey to a saucepan sprayed with a non-stick spray.
2. Cook the turkey over medium flame until it turns brown. Get rid of any grease.
3. Mix the salsa in well. For 2-3 mins, cook the turkey and salsa.
4. Put the eggs in the saucepan and cover it for 7-9 mins, or until the eggs are done the way you like. I cooked mine for the full 9 mins because I like my yolks cooked all through.

Nutrition Information:
Calories: 160kcal, Protein: 24g, Carbohydrates: 3g, Fats: 6g

Total Servings: 3
Difficulty: Easy
Preparation Time: 10 minutes
Cook Time: 35 minutes
Total Time: 45 minutes

RICOTTA, TOMATO & SPINACH FRITTATA

Ingredients

- 1 tbsp olive oil
- 1 large onion, sliced
- 10.5 oz. cherry tomatoes
- 3.5 oz. spinach leaves
- a small handful of basil leaves
- 3.5 oz. ricotta
- 6 eggs, beaten
- salad to serve

Directions

1. Adjust oven temperature to 392F. Heat the oil in a stainless steel skillet and sauté the onion for 5-6 mins, until softened and golden brown. To soften the tomatoes, add them and mix for 1 min.
2. Remove the skillet, add the spinach leaves and basil, and toss to wilt. Transfer the ingredients to a rectangu- lar baking pan that has been buttered. Spread ricotta in small dollops over the vegetables.
3. Season and thoroughly beat the eggs, then pour them over the vegetables and cheese. Cook in the oven for at least 20-25 mins or until brown and firm. Serve with a side salad.

Nutrition Information:
: Calories: 236kcal, Protein: 16g, Carbohydrates: 7g, Fats: 16g

Total Servings: 1
Difficulty: Easy
Preparation Time: 10 minutes
Cook Time: 10 minutes
Total Time: 20 minutes

PISTACHIO CRUSTED SALMON

Ingredients

- 1 – 1/3 lb salmon 1 fillet
- ½ tbsp dijon mustard coarse ground
- ½ heaping tbsp honey
- 1/3 tsp freshly squeezed lemon juice
- Pinch garlic powder optional
- 2 tbsp pistachio
- Salt and pepper to taste

Directions

1. Preheat oven to 400F. Mix the Dijon mustard, lemon juice, honey, garlic powder, salt, and pepper in a bowl.
2. Coat the salmon on all sides with the mustard mixture using a paintbrush or fingertips.
3. Place the salmon in an oven-safe dish or baking sheet and coated with parchment paper or avocado oil. In a food blender, pulse the pistachios a few times, or crush them in a Ziploc bag with a rolling pin or the bottom of a saucepan until they are in small pieces and chunks.
4. Spread the pistachios evenly over the salmon. Bake the pistachio-crusted salmon for 9-12 mins in a pre- heated oven, depending on the thickness of the salmon fillets.

Nutrition Information:
C: Calories: 298kcal, Protein: 27g, Carbohydrates: 8g, Fats: 15g

---

Total Servings: 1
Difficulty: Easy
Preparation Time: 8 minutes
Cook Time: 12 minutes
Total Time: 20 minutes

THAI PEANUT CHICKEN CURRY

Ingredients

- 1/3 lb of chicken breast
- ¾ tbsp arrowroot flour * + 2 tbsp water
- ½ tbsp creamy peanut butte
- 3 tbsp unsweetened almond milk
- 1 tbsp red curry paste
- ¾ tbsp fresh ginger minced
- ¾ tbsp cooking oil
- Salt and pepper to taste

Directions

1. Cut the chicken breasts into 1-inch cubes. Mix the arrowroot flour, water, and salt to taste in a large bowl.
2. Put the chicken in the mix to soak. Set your Instant Pot to saute, and then turn it on.
3. Put one tbsp of oil in the Instant Pot and heat it until it shimmers. Cook the bell peppers for a few mins or until they soften.
4. Put the minced ginger and red curry paste into the Instant Pot. Cook for 30 secs while you stir.
5. Add peanut butter and coconut milk and mix well. Mix in the chicken, a few dashes of cayenne pepper if you want, and the rest of the salt to taste. Close the lid. Cook under high pressure for 12 mins. Once done, do a quick release.
6. Serve with either Jasmine rice or cauliflower rice, and enjoy!

Nutrition Information:
: Calories: 298kcal, Protein: 27g, Carbohydrates: 8g, Fats: 15g

GARLIC BUTTER SHRIMP WITH SPINACH AND FETA

Total Servings: 1
Difficulty: Medium
Preparation Time: 5 minutes
Cook Time: 20 minutes
Total Time: 25 minutes

Ingredients

- ¼ lb shrimp raw, peeled, deveined.
- ¼ tsp seasoned salt
- ¼ tsp extra-virgin olive oil
- 1 garlic clove peeled and minced
- pinch crushed red pepper
- 1 tbsp fresh herbs, mint, and oregano
- ¼ juice lemon
- 2 tbsp stock
- 1.25 oz. spinach cleaned
- 1 oz. feta
- ½ tbsp butter cut into small cube
- 1 cup cauliflower rice prepared

Directions

1. Place shrimp in a strainer and rinse them under cold water while you prepare the remaining ingredients. After defrosting the shrimp:
2. Combine them with a tsp of seasoned salt.
3. In a large skillet heated over high heat with olive oil, sauté the shrimp for two minutes in a single layer.
4. Invert the shrimp.
5. Reduce the heat to moderate and add the garlic and red pepper flakes; cook for 30 secs before adding the stock and stirring to incorporate.
6. Cook the spinach and herbs for 2 mins while stirring. Add the juice of a lemon. Transfer the shrimp to one side of the pan and add the butter one at a time, whisking until it melts.
7. If necessary, turn the pan to move some of the fluid to the side where the butter is being whisked. Continue until all of the butter has been incorporated. When all of the butter has been mixed, combine all ingredients. Remove the dish from the heat and sprinkle the feta cheese on top. Serve this over canned cauliflower rice. Serve it over pasta.

Nutrition Information:
Calories: 273kcal, Protein: 23g, Carbohydrates: 3g, Fats: 5g

SEARED TILAPIA WITH SPIRALIZED ZUCCHINI

Total Servings: 1
Difficulty: Medium
Preparation Time: 5 minutes
Cook Time: 25 minutes
Total Time: 30 minutes

Ingredients

- 6 oz. zucchini
- ½ tbsp. olive oil, divided
- kosher salt and pepper to taste
- 2 small fillets of tilapia (170g)
- ¼ lemon, thinly sliced and seeded
- ½ cloves garlic, thinly sliced
- ¼ tbsp. capers
- 2 tbsp. fresh flat-leaf parsley, chopped

Directions

1. Preheat oven to 475F. Line a big sheet pan with a reusable baking mat or parchment paper.
2. Using a spiralizer, spiralize zucchini or slice zucchini into thin ribbons. Transfer zucchini to the prepared bak- ing sheet; stir oil, salt, and pepper.
3. Roast 15 min. Increase the heat to broil and continue cooking for 3-4 mins or until golden brown; in the inter- im, heat ½ tbsp of oil in a large iron skillet over normal heat.
4. Season fish with a pinch of salt&pepper and cook for 2-3 mins per side or until opaque throughout.
5. Place onto plates. Add the remaining oil, lemon, garlic, and capers to the skillet and heat, turning regularly, until the garlic is golden brown and soft. Toss with parsley, then serve zucchini beside tilapia.

Nutrition Information:
Calories: 292kcal, Protein: 37g, Carbohydrates: 8g, Fats: 13g

Total Servings: 1
Difficulty: Medium
Preparation Time: 10 minutes
Cook Time: 25 minutes
Total Time: 35 minutes

TURKEY TENDERLOIN

Ingredients

- 4 oz. turkey tenderloin (yes, it's the standard recommended serving)
- ½ tbsp olive oil
- 1 tsp Italian seasoning
- 1/8 tsp dried sage
- 1/8 tsp garlic powder
- 1/8 tsp kosher salt
- Pinch of freshly ground black pepper
- 1 tbsp butter

Directions

1. Put a 10-inch cast-iron skillet on the middle rack of the oven and heat it to 450F. The pan will heat up at the same time as the oven.
2. With oven mitts, take the pan out of the oven and add olive oil. Turn the pan around so the oil covers the whole bottom.
3. Mix the sage, garlic powder, salt, and pepper (black) in a small bowl with the Italian seasoning.
4. Sprinkle the seasoning mix on both sides of the turkey and rub the spices with your fingers. Put the tender- loin in the pan and, using oven mitts, put the pan back in the oven for 10 mins.
5. After 10 mins, take the pan out of the oven and flip the turkey over with tongs. Turn the oven to 400F, and roast for another 15 mins. Take the pan out of the range.
6. Put butter on top of the turkey and cover the pan with a large plate, lid, or foil. Give the turkey 15 mins to rest before you serve it. Get rid of the foil. Slice the turkey and pour the butter sauce over it. Enjoy hot

Nutrition Information:
Calories: 245kcal, Protein: 30g, Carbohydrates: 5g, Fats: 18g

DESSERTS RECIPES

Total Servings: 14
Difficulty: Easy
Preparation Time: 8 minutes
Cook Time: 17 minutes
Total Time: 25 minutes

SHORTBREAD COOKIES

Ingredients

- ¼ tsp. monk fruit sweetener
- 4 tbsp. softened butter
- 2 large eggs
- 1 tsp. vanilla extract
- 2 cups almond flour

Directions

1. Set your oven temperature range to 350F to preheat. Arrange the baking sheet with baking paper. In the large bowl, beat the first butter with sweetener until fluffy and creamy, then beat in eggs (add one by one) and leftover ingredients.
2. Knead the dough until everything looks smooth. Split the dough into 12-14 balls and flatten each with your palm to make a cookie. Place the cookies on the arranged baking sheet and bake for 17 minutes. Then remove, cool thoroughly, serve and enjoy.

Nutrition Information:
Calories: 174kcal, Proteins: 7g, Carbohydrate: 5g, Fat: 14g

Total Servings: 12
Difficulty: Easy
Preparation Time: 8 minutes
Cook Time: 7 minutes
Total Time: 15 minutes

PUMPKIN PIE SPICES COOKIES

Ingredients

- ¾ cup coconut flour
- ½ cup pumpkin puree
- 3 tsp. pumpkin pie spice
- 1½ cups peanut butter
- ¼ tsp. liquid monk fruit sweetener

Directions

1. Set your oven temperature range to 375F to preheat. Arrange the baking sheet with baking paper. Melt the butter, then mix in monk fruit sweetener. Then beat in leftover ingredients.
2. Knead the dough until everything looks smooth. Split the dough into 12 portions and flatten each with your palm to make a cookie. Place the cookies on the arranged baking sheet and bake for 5-7 minutes. Then remove, cool thoroughly, serve and enjoy.

Nutrition Information:
: Calories: 208kcal, Proteins: 8g, Carbohydrate: 8g, Fat: 16g

Total Servings: 12
Difficulty: Easy
Preparation Time: 10 minutes
Cook Time: 10 minutes
Total Time: 20 minutes

COCONUT FLOUR COOKIES

Ingredients

- ½ cup coconut flour
- ¼ tsp. stevia
- ¼ tsp. baking soda
- 1/3 cup melted butter
- 3 large eggs
- 1 cup unsweetened chocolate chips

Directions

1. Set your oven temperature range to 350F to preheat. Arrange the baking sheet with baking paper. Gather the dry elements in the large bowl. Melt the butter, then mix in sweetener. Then beat in leftover liquid ingre- dients.
2. Add liquid mixture (add in portions) to dry mixture bowl and knead the dough until everything looks smooth. Split the dough into 10-12 portions and flatten each with your palm to make a cookie.
3. Place the cookies on the arranged baking sheet and bake for 10 minutes. Then remove, cool thoroughly, serve and enjoy.

Nutrition Information:
Calories: 166kcal, Proteins: 7g, Carbohydrate: 3g, Fat: 14g

Total Servings: 20
Difficulty: Easy
Preparation Time: 9 minutes
Cook Time: 6 minutes
Total Time: 15 minutes

SHREDDED COCONUT COOKIES

Ingredients

- 2½ cups unsweetened shredded coconut
- 1/3 cup coconut oil
- ½ cup almond flour
- ¼ tsp. liquid monk fruit sweetener

Directions

1. Set your oven temperature range to 275F to preheat. Arrange the baking sheet with baking paper. Mix all the ingredients in the high-powder blender.
2. When finely done, remove and split the dough into 20 balls and flatten each with your palm to make the cookie. Place the cookies on the arranged baking sheet and bake for 4-6 minutes.
3. Then remove, cool thoroughly, serve and enjoy.

Nutrition Information:
Calories: 133kcal, Proteins: 1g, Carbohydrate: 3g, Fat: 13g

Total Servings: 18
Difficulty: Easy
Preparation Time: 10 minutes
Cook Time: 15 minutes
Total Time: 25 minutes

LEMON COOKIES SWEETS

Ingredients

- 2 cups superfine almond flour
- ¼ tsp. salt
- ½ tsp. liquid monk fruit sweetener
- 2 tbsp. lemon zest
- 2 large egg whites
- 1 tsp. lemon extract
- 2 drops of yellow food color
- 1 tbsp. monk fruit sweetener powder

Directions

1. Set your oven temperature range to 350F to preheat. Arrange the baking sheet with baking paper. Mix the dry elements (except powder sweetener) in a large bowl.
2. Gather liquid ingredients in the other bowl. Add liquid mixture (add in portions) to dry mixture bowl and knead the dough until everything looks smooth. Split the dough into 18 balls and flatten each with your palm to make a cookie.
3. Place the cookies on the arranged baking sheet, sprinkle monk fruit sweetener powder over the cookies and bake for 15 minutes. Then remove, cool thoroughly, serve, and enjoy.

Nutrition Information:
Calories: 78kcal, Proteins: 3g, Carbohydrate: 3g, Fat: 6g

Total Servings: 8
Difficulty: Easy
Preparation Time: 10 minutes
Cook Time: 15 minutes
Total Time: 25 minutes

KETO CHOCOLATE CAKE

Ingredients

- 1½ cups almond flour
- 4 tbsp. unsweetened cocoa powder
- 2 tbsp. regular cocoa
- 2¼ tsp. baking powder
- ½ tsp. salt
- 1/3 cup water
- 3 eggs
- ¼ tsp. stevia
- ½ tbsp. pure vanilla extract

Directions

1. Set your oven temperature range to 350F to preheat. Arrange the cake pan with parchment paper and set it aside. Mix all the elements in the large bowl. Pour the cake batter into the arranged cake pan.
2. Give some jerks to the cake pan to smooth the upper surface. Bake for 14 mins until the tester stick insert comes out clean. If you want a double-layer cake, then double the recipe.
3. Then remove, cool before slicing, then frost with your desired topping, serve, and enjoy.

Nutrition Information:
Calories: 133kcal, Proteins: 7g, Carbohydrate: 6g, Fat: 9g

Total Servings: 16
Difficulty: Medium
Preparation Time: 10 minutes
Cook Time: 25 minutes
Total Time: 35 minutes

LOW CARB VANILLA CAKE

Ingredients

- 1½ cups almond flour
- ½ cup coconut flour
- 2 tsp. baking powder
- ¼ tsp. salt
- ¾ cup butter
- ½ tsp. stevia
- 4 large eggs
- ½ cup vegan milk (almond)
- 1 tsp. vanilla extract

Directions

1. Set your oven temperature range to 350F to preheat. Arrange the two cake pans with parchment paper and set them aside. Beat butter and stevia until it comes in a fluffy form. Add eggs (one by one), mix well, then add milk and vanilla and beat well.
2. Add leftover ingredients and mix well. Now pour the cake batter into the two arranged cake pans. Give some jerks to the cake pans to smooth the upper surface.
3. Bake for 22-25 mins until the tester stick insert comes out clean. Then remove, cool before slicing, then frost with your desired topping (it must be keto), serve, and enjoy.

Nutrition Information:
Calories: 180kcal, Proteins: 4g, Carbohydrate: 5g, Fat: 16g

Total Servings: 12
Difficulty: Medium
Preparation Time: 16 minutes
Cook Time: 24 minutes
Total Time: 40 minutes

CREAM CHEESE POUND CAKE

Ingredients

- 1¼ cups almond flour
- 1 tsp. baking powder
- ¼ tsp. salt
- 4 tbsp. unsalted butter
- ¼ tsp. liquid stevia
- ½ cup full-fat cream cheese
- 1 tsp. vanilla extract
- 4 eggs

Directions

1. Set your oven temperature range to 350F to preheat. Arrange the pound cake loaf pan with parchment pa- per and set it aside. Mix flour, baking powder, and salt, and set aside. Beat butter and stevia until it comes in a fluffy form, then add cream cheese and vanilla.
2. Mix the dry and liquid ingredients in the bowl, then add eggs (add one by one) and mix well. Mix until smooth form batter. Now pour the cake batter into the loaf cake pan. Give some jerks to the loaf pan to smooth the upper surface.
3. Bake for 21-24 mins until the tester stick insert comes out clean. Then remove, cool before slicing, serve, and enjoy.

Nutrition Information:
Calories: 138kcal, Proteins: 3g, Carbohydrate: 9g, Fat: 10g

Total Servings: 6
Difficulty: Hard
Preparation Time: 10 minutes
Cook Time: 40 minutes
Total Time: 50 minutes

BLUEBERRY DUMP CAKE

Ingredients

- 1 cup almond flour
- ½ cup monk fruit sweetener
- ¼ cup butter, melted
- 2 cups fresh or frozen blueberries
- 1 tsp. lemon juice
- 1 tsp. cinnamon

Directions

1. Set your oven heat range to 350°F to preheat. Use butter or non-stick spray to grease a 9x9-inch baking dish. Mix the almond flour, ¼ cup sweetener, and butter (melted) in a medium bowl until everything is well- mixed.
2. Spread the mixture evenly on the bottom of the dish set up for baking. Mix the blueberries, lemon juice, cin- namon, and ¼ cup of sweetener in a separate bowl.
3. Spread the blueberry mixture on top of the crust in an even layer. Bake for 35-40 minutes until the blueber- ries are bubbling and the top is golden brown. Wait at least 10 minutes before serving the cake.

Nutrition Information:
Calories: 139kcal, Proteins: 2g, Carbohydrate: 8g, Fat: 11g

Total Servings: 8
Difficulty: Hard
Preparation Time: 20 minutes
Cook Time: 80 minutes
Total Time: 1 hr 40 mins

DIABETIC CHEESECAKE

Ingredients

- ½ cup almond flour
- ½ cup coconut flour
- 4 tbsp. shredded coconut
- ½ cup melted butter
- 1 cup softened cream cheese
- 1 cup softened fat-free sour cream
- 1 tbsp. liquid stevia
- 2 tsp. pure vanilla extract
- 3 large eggs, not chill

Directions

1. Set your oven temperature range to 300F to preheat. Arrange the oven baking pan with aluminum foil and set it aside. Mix the almond flour with coconut flour, shredded coconut, and melted butter in the large bowl.
2. Press the flour mixture to the bottom of the foiled cake pan. In the other large bowl, beat the leftover ingre- dients (ensure while adding eggs add one by one) until they come in a smooth form. Now pour the liquid mixture over the dry mixture crust and bake for 60-80 mins.
3. Check the cake's doneness using a tester stick; insert the tester stick, and it comes out clean. Then remove and cool before slicing. Serve, and enjoy.

Nutrition Information:
Calories: 282kcal, Proteins: 6.3g, Carbohydrate: 7.3g, Fat: 25.3g

CHOCOLATE MUG CAKE

Total Servings: 1
Difficulty: Easy
Preparation Time: 03 minutes
Cook Time: 02 minutes
Total Time: 05 minutes

Ingredients

- 2 tbsp. softened butter
- 1/8 tsp. liquid stevia
- 1 large egg
- 3-4 drops of vanilla extract
- 2 tbsp. almond flour
- 1 tsp. coconut flour
- 2 tbsp. cocoa powder, unsweetened
- ¼ tsp. baking powder

Directions

1. In the microwave mug, add butter with liquid stevia, mix them well, then microwave for 30 seconds. Add egg with vanilla extract drops and stir well to combine.
2. Now stir the leftover ingredients into the mug until a smooth form appears. Microwave for 40-60 seconds (at 1000W), then remove and cool completely. Top with your desired low-carb frosting. Serve and enjoy

Nutrition Information:
Calories: 220cal, Proteins: 6g, Carbohydrate: 8.5g, Fat: 18g

CARROT CAKE WITH CREAM CHEESE FROSTING

Total Servings: 12
Difficulty: Medium
Preparation Time: 15 minutes
Cook Time: 35 minutes
Total Time: 50 minutes

Ingredients

- Carrot Cake:
- 4 medium Eggs
- 2 tsp. vanilla extract
- 1/3 cup olive oil
- ½ tsp. liquid stevia
- 2 cups almond flour
- 2 tsp. baking soda
- 2 tbsp. coconut flour
- ½ tsp. baking powder
- 1 tsp. nutmeg powder
- 3 tsp. cinnamon powder
- Pinch of salt
- 1 cup melted butter
- ½ cup chopped pecans
- 2 cups shredded carrots
- Cream Cheese Frosting:
- 1 cup softened cream cheese
- ¼ tsp. powder stevia
- ½ cup softened (not melted) butter
- 1 tsp. vanilla extract
- 1/3 cup heavy whipped cream

Directions

1. Set your oven temperature range to 350F to preheat. Arrange the two cake pans with parchment paper; mix egg, olive oil, and vanilla in the large. Mix in dry cake batter elements (except carrot and pecans); now add melted butter with shredded carrot and chopped pecans.
2. Pour the carrot cake batter into arranged cake pans and bake for 30-35 mins. Check the cake's doneness using a tester stick; insert the tester stick, and it comes out clean.
3. Meanwhile, prepare the cake frosting, and blend the frosting elements into the large bowl. Blend until a fluffy and smooth form is achieved. Then remove the cake, and cool completely before slicing. Top with frosting, serve and enjoy.

Nutrition Information:
Calories: 444cal, Proteins: 8g, Carbohydrate: 4g, Fat: 44g

Total Servings: 1
Difficulty: Easy
Preparation Time: 03 minutes
Cook Time: 02 minutes
Total Time: 05 minutes

VANILLA MUG CAKE

Ingredients

- 2 tbsp. almond flour
- 1 tbsp. coconut flour
- 3 tsp. melted butter
- ¼ tsp. baking powder
- 1 medium egg
- 1/8 tsp. liquid stevia
- 1 tsp. vanilla extract

Directions

1. In the microwave mug, add butter with liquid stevia, mix them well, then microwave for 30 seconds. Add egg with vanilla extract drops and stir well to combine.
2. Now stir the leftover ingredients into the mug and mix until a smooth form appears. Microwave for 80 sec- onds at 900W, then remove and cool completely. Top with your desired low-carb frosting. Serve and enjoy.

Nutrition Information:
Calories: 267kcal, Proteins: 10g, Carbohydrate: 5g, Fat: 23g

Total Servings: 12
Difficulty: Medium
Preparation Time: 13 minutes
Cook Time: 27 minutes
Total Time: 40 minutes

ALMOND FLOUR FUDGY BROWNIE

Ingredients

- 1½ cups almond flour
- 1 tsp. baking powder
- ½ tsp. salt
- 5 tbsp. softened butter
- 1¼ tsp. stevia powder
- ¾ cup unsweetened cocoa powder
- 3 large eggs
- 1 tsp. vanilla extract
- ½ cup chocolate chips (optional)

Directions

1. Set your oven temperature range to 350F to preheat. Arrange the brownie pan with parchment paper. Mix the dry elements in a medium bowl and set aside. Beat softened butter, vanilla extract, and eggs in a small bowl. Add the dry and liquid mixture to the large and mix with spatula.
2. Transfer the brownie mixture to the brownie pan and give some jerks to the pan to smooth the upper sur- face. Bake for 25-27 mins until the tester stick insert comes out clean. Then remove, cool before slicing, cut into slices, serve, and enjoy.

Nutrition Information:
Calories: 125kcal, Proteins: 6g, Carbohydrate: 5g, Fat: 9g

Total Servings: 8
Difficulty: Medium
Preparation Time: 12 minutes
Cook Time: 28 minutes
Total Time: 40 minutes

COCONUT FLOUR BROWNIES

Ingredients

- ¾ cup pure peanut butter
- 2/3 cup hot water
- ½ tsp. stevia powder
- 3 tbsp. ground flaxseed meal
- 1 tsp. vanilla extract
- ¾ cup cocoa powder, unsweetened
- 2 tbsp. coconut flour
- ¼ tsp. baking soda

Directions

1. Set your oven temperature range to 325F to preheat. Brush the brownie pan with cooking spray lightly. Mix the dry elements in a medium bowl and set aside. Beat peanut butter, vanilla extract, and hot water in a small bowl.
2. Add the dry and liquid mixture to the large bowl and mix well until crumbly form produce. Transfer the brownie mixture to the lightly greased pan and give some jerks to the pan to smooth the upper surface.
3. Bake for 24-28 mins until the tester stick insert comes out clean. Then remove, cool before slicing, cut into slices, serve, and enjoy.

Nutrition Information:
Calories: 232kcal, Proteins: 9.4g, Carbohydrate: 13g, Fat: 15.8g

Total Servings: 12
Difficulty: Easy
Preparation Time: 10 minutes
Cook Time: 20 minutes
Total Time: 30 minutes

FUDGY KETO BROWNIES

Ingredients

- ¾ cup vegan butter spread
- ½ cup oat fiber
- ½ tsp. baking powder
- ¼ tsp. salt
- ½ cup chocolate chips, sugar-free
- 4 tbsp. unsweetened cocoa powder
- 1 cup allulose
- 3 medium eggs
- 1 tsp. vanilla extract

Directions

1. Set your oven temperature range to 350F to preheat. Arrange the brownie pan with aluminum foil. Micro-wave the chocolate chips, then combine the liquid ingredients. Mix the dry elements in a medium bowl and set aside.
2. Add the dry and liquid mixture to the large bowl and mix well until crumbly form produce. Transfer the brownie mixture to the arranged aluminum foil pan and give some jerks to the pan to smooth the upper surface.
3. Bake for 15-20 mins until the tester stick insert comes out clean. Then remove, cool before slicing, cut into slices, serve, and enjoy.

Nutrition Information:
Calories: 137kcal, Protein: 1.6g, Carbohydrate: 4.6g, Fat: 12.1g

Total Servings: 24
Difficulty: Easy
Preparation Time: 10 minutes
Cook Time: 25 minutes
Total Time: 35 minutes

SUGAR-FREE CHOCOLATE BROWNIES

Ingredients

- 1 cup almond flour
- 1 tsp. baking powder
- ¾ cup cocoa powder, unsweetened
- 1 tsp. liquid stevia
- 1 cup vegan butter spread
- 3 medium eggs
- 2 tsp. vanilla extract
- 1 cup of chocolate chips, unsweetened

Directions

1. Set your oven temperature range to 325F to preheat. Arrange the brownie pan with parchment paper that goes overhead the pan. Mix the liquid elements in a medium bowl and set aside. Mix the dry elements in another medium bowl and set aside.
2. Add the dry and liquid mixture to the dough-making machine bowl and mix well until a smooth form ap- pears. Transfer the brownie mixture to the paper-arranged pan, give some jerks to the pan to smooth the upper surface, or do it with a rubber spatula.
3. Bake for 20-25 mins until the tester stick insert comes out clean. Then remove, cool before slicing, cut into slices, serve, and enjoy.

Nutrition Information:
Calories: 137kcal, Protein: 1.6g, Carbohydrate: 4.6g, Fat: 12.1g

Total Servings: 8
Difficulty: Medium
Preparation Time: 10 minutes
Cook Time: 30 minutes
Total Time: 40 minutes

OAT FLOUR BROWNIES

Ingredients

- 1 cup unsweetened chocolate chips
- 1/3 cup almond butter
- 4 tbsp. oat flour
- 3 tbsp. cacao powder, unsweetened
- ½ tsp. stevia powder
- 1 tsp. baking powder
- 2/3 cup water

Directions

1. Set your oven temperature range to 375F to preheat. Arrange the brownie pan with parchment paper that goes overhead the pan. Melt the chocolate chips in the microwave and mix in almond butter and unsweet- ened chocolate chips.
2. Add oat flour with stevia powder and mix again. Mix in baking powder and water until a smooth form ap- pears. Transfer the brownie mixture to the paper-arranged pan, give some jerks to the pan to smooth the upper surface, or do it with a rubber spatula.
3. Bake for 30 mins until the tester stick insert comes out clean. Then remove, cool before slicing, cut into slic- es, serve, and enjoy.

Nutrition Information:
: Calories: 187kcal, Protein: 5g, Carbohydrate: 12g, Fat: 13g

Total Servings: 16
Difficulty: Medium
Preparation Time: 10 minutes
Cook Time: 25 minutes
Total Time: 35 minutes

SUGAR- FREE COFFEE CHOCOLAT BROWNIES

Ingredients

- 8 oz. unsweetened chocolate chips
- 3 tsp. instant coffee
- ½ cup avocado oil
- ½ cup butter
- 2 large eggs
- 1 yolk of a large egg
- 2 tsp. vanilla extract
- 1 tsp. liquid stevia
- 4 tbsp. heavy cream
- ¼ cup monk fruit sweetener
- 4 tbsp. coconut flour
- 1 scoop of protein powder
- 4 tbsp. unsweetened cocoa powder
- ½ tsp. baking powder
- ¼ tsp. salt

Directions

1. Set your oven temperature range to 350F to preheat. Brush the baking pan with some butter. Melt the choc- olate chips and add to the dough mixing bowl with butter, oil, eggs, egg yolk, heavy cream, and liquid stevia.
2. Then add the leftover ingredients and mix until soft and smooth peak form. Place the brownie mixture in the pan and smooth the upper surface with a rubber spatula.
3. Bake for 21-25 mins until the tester stick insert comes out clean. Then remove, cool before slicing, cut into slices, serve, and enjoy.

Nutrition Information:
Calories: 153kcal, Protein: 5g, Carbohydrate: 4g, Fat: 13g

Total Servings: 9
Difficulty: Medium
Preparation Time: 10 minutes
Cook Time: 25 minutes
Total Time: 35 minutes

PROTEIN LOADED BROWNIES

Ingredients

- ¾ cup butter
- ½ cup sugar-free chocolate chips
- 1 cup erythritol sweetener
- 1 cup unsweetened cocoa powder
- ½ cup blanched almond flour
- 2 scoops of unflavored protein powder
- Pinch of salt
- 4 large eggs

Directions

1. Set your oven temperature range to 350F to preheat. Brush the baking pan with some melted butter. Melt the chocolate chips, add butter to it and mix well. Then add the leftover ingredients (except eggs) and mix well.
2. Add eggs (add one by one); mix again until soft and smooth peak form. Place the brownie mixture in the pan and smooth the upper surface with a rubber spatula.
3. Bake for 23-25 mins until the tester stick insert comes out clean. Then remove, cool before slicing, cut into slices, serve, and enjoy.

Nutrition Information:
Calories: 242kcal, Protein: 11g, Carbohydrate: 9g, Fat: 18g

Total Servings: 8 scones
Difficulty: Medium
Preparation Time: 12 minutes
Cook Time: 23 minutes
Total Time: 35 minutes

TAPIOCA AND ALMOND FLOUR SCONES

Ingredients

- ¼ cup tapioca flour
- 2½ cups fine almond flour
- ¼ tsp. stevia
- 2½ tsp. baking powder
- ¼ tsp. salt
- 4 tbsp. melted coconut oil
- 4 tbsp. water
- 1 tsp. vanilla extract

Directions

1. Set your oven temperature range to 325F to preheat. Mix the dry elements in a medium bowl and set aside. Beat melted butter, vanilla extract, and water in a small bowl. Add the dry and liquid mixture to the dough-making machine or knead with your hands.
2. After making the dough, roll them flattened and cut the scones (in your desired shape). Bake for 21-23 mins until golden. Cool over a steel wire rack, serve and enjoy.

Nutrition Information:
Calories: 120kcal, Proteins: 1.9g, Carbohydrate: 5.8g, Fat: 11.2g

Total Servings: 8
Difficulty: Medium
Preparation Time: 09 minutes
Cook Time: 21 minutes
Total Time: 30 minutes

KETO BLUEBERRY SCONES

Ingredients

- ¼ cup coconut flour
- 3 tbsp. erythritol
- ½ tsp. baking powder
- ¼ tsp. salt
- 4 tbsp. unsweetened almond milk
- 1 cup almond flour, blanched
- 2 tbsp. melted coconut oil
- 1 large egg
- 1 tsp. vanilla extract
- ½ cup fresh blueberries
Glaze:
- 3 tsp. coconut oil
- 1 tsp. erythritol sweetener powder
- 2 tbsp. mashed fresh blueberries

Directions

1. Set your oven temperature range to 350F to preheat. Arrange the baking sheet with baking pepper. Mix the dry elements in a medium bowl and set aside. Beat melted oil, vanilla extract, and egg in a small bowl.
2. Add the dry and liquid mixture to the dough-making machine or knead with your hands. After making the dough, roll it flattened (using a rolling pin) and cut it into 8 scones (in your desired shape). Bake for 19-21 mins until golden. Cool over a steel wire rack.
3. Blend the glaze elements in the blender, then walk through the fine mesh sieve to discard the skin. Pour glaze over cool scones. Serve and enjoy.

Nutrition Information:
Calories: 169kcal, Proteins: 5g, Carbohydrate: 8g, Fat: 13g

OAT AND COCONUT FLOUR SCONES

Total Servngs: 6 scones
Difficulty: Medium
Preparation Time: 10 minutes
Cook Time: 15 minutes
Total Time: 25 minutes

Ingredients

- 1½ cups rolled oats
- 4 tbsp. coconut flour
- ¼ tsp. stevia
- 1½ tsp. baking powder
- ¼ tsp. salt
- 3 tbsp. coconut oil
- ½ cup ice water

Directions

1. Set your oven temperature range to 375F to preheat. Arrange the baking sheet with parchment paper. Turn oats into fine flour in a high-power blender. Mix the dry elements in the dough and knead the bowl. Cut cold oil into pieces and add to the bowl, then add water and knead until the required dough is found.
2. After making the dough, roll it flattened (using a rolling pin) and cut it into 6 scones (in your desired shape). Bake for 11-15 mins until golden. Cool over a steel wire rack, serve and enjoy.

Nutrition Information:
Calories: 93kcal, Proteins: 1g, Carbohydrate: 6g, Fat: 7.4g

GREEK YOGURT CHOCOLATE FUDGE POPS

Total Servings: 12 Pops
Difficulty: Easy
Preparation Time: 15 minutes
Cook Time: 5 hr
Total Time: 5 hr 20 mintes

Ingredients

- 1 1/2 cups semi-sweet chocolate chips
- 1 cup chocolate almond milk, cow's milk, or non-dairy milk of your choice
- 2 teaspoons vanilla extract
- 1 1/2 cups Vanilla Greek Yogurt

Directions

1. In a small saucepan over medium-low heat melt the chocolate chips, stirring constantly, until completely melted.
2. Add in the milk and increase the heat to medium; bring to a gentle simmer, stirring constantly, then remove from heat.
3. Cool for 5 minutes. Whisk in vanilla and Greek yogurt; mix well until completely smooth. Place a fine-mesh sieve over a large bowl (preferably one with a spout) and pour the chocolate mixture through the sieve.
4. Pour the strained chocolate liquid into the Popsicle molds and place them in the freezer for 1 hour. At this point remove the pops from the freezer and insert the Popsicle sticks in. Freeze for 5 hours, or until hard.

Nutrition Information:
: Calories: 118kcal, Proteins: 3g, Carbohydrate: 9g, Fat: 8g

Total Servings: 8 scones
Difficulty: Medium
Preparation Time: 12 minutes
Cook Time: 18 minutes
Total Time: 30 minutes

MAPLE PECAN SCONES

Ingredients

- ½ cup chopped pecans
- 1¼ cups almond flour
- 6 tbsp. coconut flour
- Pinch of salt
- ¾ tsp. baking powder
- 3 tbsp. melted butter
- 6 tbsp. keto maple syrup
- 1½ tsp. vanilla extract
- 1 large egg
- 1 egg white of jumbo egg

Directions

1. Set your oven temperature range to 350F to preheat. Arrange the baking sheet with baking paper. Mix the dry elements (except chopped pecans) in the dough knead machine or large kitchen bowl.
2. Mix the liquid elements in another bowl and add slowly to the dry elements. Knead well, add chopped pe- cans, roll the dough in a flattened shape (using a rolling pin) and cut into 8 scones (in your desired shape).
3. Bake for 15-18 mins until golden. Cool over a steel wire rack, top your favorite filling, serve, and enjoy.

Nutrition Information:
Calories: 138kcal, Proteins: 4g, Carbohydrate: 8g, Fat: 10g

Total Servings: 3 scones
Difficulty: Medium
Preparation Time: 10 minutes
Cook Time: 25 minutes
Total Time: 35 minutes

KETO EGGLESS SCONES

Ingredients

- 4 tbsp. lupin flour
- 1 scoop of whey protein powder, unsweetened
- ½ tsp. xanthan gum
- ½ tsp. baking powder
- Pinch of salt
- ½ cup water

Directions

1. Set your oven temperature range to 375F to preheat. Arrange the baking sheet with baking paper. Mix the dry elements in the dough-kneading machine or large kitchen bowl. Mix the liquid elements in another bowl and add slowly to the dry elements.
2. Knead well, roll the dough in a flattened shape (using a rolling pin), and split it into 3 scones. Bake for 25 mins until golden. Cool, serve, and enjoy.

Nutrition Information:
: Calories: 43cal, Proteins: 7g, Carbohydrate: 2.6g, Fat: 0.5g

Total Servngs: 12 scones
Difficulty: Medium
Preparation Time: 13 minutes
Cook Time: 22 minutes
Total Time: 40 minutes

APPLE-SAUCE CINNAMON SCONES

Ingredients

- ¾ cup coconut flour
- ¾ cup quinoa flour
- ¼ cup tapioca starch
- 1 tsp. baking powder
- ¼ tsp. baking soda
- 2 tsp. psyllium husk powder
- ½ tbsp. cinnamon powder
- ¼ tsp. ground nutmeg
- ¼ tsp. stevia powder
- 2 tbsp. coconut oil
- ¾ cup unsweetened applesauce
- ½ cup water

Directions

1. Set your oven temperature range to 350F to preheat. Arrange the baking sheet with baking paper. Mix the dry elements in the dough-kneading machine or large kitchen bowl. Mix the liquid elements in another bowl and add slowly to the dry elements.
2. Knead well, roll the dough in a flattened shape (using a rolling pin) and split it into 12 scones (divide the dough into two parts).
3. Place the scones (give a small distance between them) on the baking sheet, brush with applesauce, and bake for 22 mins until golden. Cool for 5 mins over a steel rack, serve and enjoy.

Nutrition Information:
Calories: 43cal, Proteins: 1.3g, Carbohydrate: 11g, Fat: 2.9g

Total Servings: 4 Pops
Difficulty: Easy
Preparation Time: 10 minutes
Cook Time: 00 hr
Total Time: 10 mintes

CREAMY BUTTERSCOTCH ICE CREAM

Ingredients

- 1 packet butterscotch pudding
- 1¾ cups almond milk, unsweetened
- ½ cup heavy whipping cream
- 2 tbsp. cream cheese
- 1 tsp. vanilla extract

Directions

1. Blend all ingredients in a food blender for 30 seconds. Pour the mixture into a Ninja Creamy pint and freeze it overnight. After overnight, put the pint in the outer container of the machine, lock it in place, and use the ice cream button to mix.
2. Once it is mixed, make a well in the middle of the ice cream if it is powdery or hard, and fill it with heavy whipping cream. Use the "mix-in" button on the machine after putting the ingredients back in.

Nutrition Information:
Calories: 159kcal, Proteins: 1g, Carbohydrate: 5g, Fat: 15g

Total Servings: 8 scones
Difficulty: Medium
Preparation Time: 12 minutes
Cook Time: 18 minutes
Total Time: 30 minutes

LOW CARB AND SUGAR ICE CREAM

Ingredients

- 1¾ cups coconut milk
- 480g double cream
- 50g keto-friendly sweetener
- 1 tsp. pure vanilla extract
- Pinch of salt

Directions

1. Chill the coconut milk in the refrigerator overnight. To make whipped coconut, put the coconut cream in a large bowl, leaving the liquid in the can, and beat it with a hand mixer until it is very creamy. Set aside.
2. Using a hand mixer or the bowl of a stand mixer, beat double cream in a separate large bowl until soft peaks form. Beat in sweetener and vanilla.
3. Mix the coconut into the whipped cream, then put the whole thing into a loaf pan. Freeze for about 5 hours or until hard.

Nutrition Information:
Calories: 331kcal, Proteins: 3g, Carbohydrate: 5g, Fat: 35g

Total Servings: 1 scones
Difficulty: Medium
Preparation Time: 10 minutes
Cook Time: 00 minutes
Total Time: 10 minutes

SOFT VANILLA PROTEIN ICE CREAM

Ingredients

- ¼ cup heavy whipping cream
- ¾ unsweetened almond milk
- ¼ tsp. liquid vanilla stevia
- 1 scoop vanilla protein powder

Directions

1. Put the thermal container for your Dash mini-ice cream maker in the freezer the day before. When making ice cream the following day, combine the 4 ingredients in a blender and process for 10–20 seconds to com- bine thoroughly.
2. Pull the thermal container from the freezer and get the machine ready. After adding the paddle and machine top, pour the mixture in. Then, let it churn for 15 to 30 minutes. Mine was 25 minutes long. Watch it near the end because the machine's top will start to sway as the liquid turns to ice cream.
3. Make sure it doesn't fall off the counter; it won't hurt anything. Scoop all the ice cream into a bowl and shut off the machine. It will partially freeze on the container walls, but don't worry. The ice cream from this batch is plentiful.
4. If you'd like, you can customize the flavor by adding keto chocolate chips, nuts, flavor extracts, etc.

Nutrition Information:
Calories: 250kcal, Proteins: 28g, Carbohydrate: 3g, Fat: 14g

SALADS RECIPES

Total Servings: 6
Difficulty: Medium
Preparation Time: 5 minutes
Cook Time: 30 minutes
Total Time: 35 minutes

CHOPPED CHICKEN SALAD

Ingredients

- Baked Chicken
- 2 lbs. boneless skinless chicken thighs
- Olive oil spray
- ½ tsp garlic powder
- ½ tsp onion powder
- ½ tsp salt and pepper (separately)
- Salad
- 3 cups chopped kale in bite-sized pieces
- 1 cup chopped Brussels sprouts, bite-sized slices
- 1 cup sliced purple cabbage
- 1sliced carrot
- 1 sliced red onion,
- 1 small, sliced stalk of fennel
- ¼ cup pomegranate seeds
- Garlic Citrus Vinaigrette
- ¼ cup extra virgin olive oil
- 1 ½ lemon, juiced
- 1 tsp salt and paper
- 1 minced garlic clove
- 1 tsp minced fennel (reserved from above)

Directions

1. Preheat oven to 375F. Spray a small pan with olive oil spray and season chicken thighs on both sides with seasonings.
2. Bake for 30 mins. Set apart and permit to cool. Prepare the salad ingredients while the chicken is baking. Get the chopped ingredients. Then cut the purple cabbage, carrot, red onion, and fennel into thin slices. Cut up the tomato. Place the ingredients in a large basin and refrigerate until required.
3. Shake all the vinaigrette ingredients vigorously in a Mason jar. Place in the refrigerator until ready for con- sumption.
4. After the chicken has cooled, cut it into bite-size pieces and sprinkle them over the salad. Drizzle on the vinaigrette and stir.

Nutrition Information:
Calories: 329kcal, Protein: 30g, Carbohydrates: 14g, Fats: 16g

---

Total Servings: 2
Difficulty: Easy
Preparation Time: 5 minutes
Cook Time: 5 minutes
Total Time: 10 minutes

COBB SALAD

Ingredients

- 8 cherry tomatoes
- 1 avocado
- 2 hard-boiled eggs
- 4 cups mixed green salad
- 4 oz. shredded chicken breast
- 2 oz. crumbled feta cheese
- ½ cup cooked bacon, crumbled

Directions

1. Cut the tomatoes and avocado into cubes. Then cut the egg into pieces. Put the mixed greens in a big bowl or plate for salad.
2. Measure the shredded chicken breast, crumbled bacon, and feta cheese.
3. On top of the gardens, make horizontal rows of tomato, avocado, egg, chicken, feta, and bacon.

Nutrition Information:
Calories: 412cal, Protein: 38g, Carbohydrates: 12g, Fats: 23g

SALMON SALAD WITH TAHINI YOGURT DRESSING

Total Servngs: 4
Difficulty: Hard
Preparation Time: 20 minutes
Cook Time: 10 minutes
Total Time: 30 minutes

Ingredients

Salmon
- 4 oz. skin-on wild-caught salmon fillets
- ½ tsp dried dill
- ½ tsp dried oregano
- ¼ tsp granulated garlic
- Sea salt and black pepper to taste
- Tahini Yogurt Dressing
- ½ cup plain nonfat Greek yogurt
- 1 tbsp tahini
- 1 ½ tsp olive oil
- 1 lemon, juiced
- ¼ tsp ground cumin
- ¼ tsp dried dill
- ¼ tsp granulated garlic
- ¼ tsp coriander
- Sea salt and black pepper to taste

Salad
- 6 cups chopped romaine lettuce 1/3 cup sliced red onion
- 1/3 cup kalamata olives 2 oz. feta cheese, cubed 1 cup diced Cucumber
- ½ cup cherry tomatoes halved
- 1 tsp olive oil
- 1 tsp red wine vinegar
- ¼ tsp dried oregano
- ¼ tsp dried dill
- Sea salt and pepper to taste

Directions

1. Prepare the grill for medium-high heat, and then oil the grates. Using a mortar and pestle or your hands, combine all of the spices for the salmon and crush them while the grill is preheating. Spread evenly across the salmon. Depending on the thickness, place the salmon flesh-side down on the grill and cook for 3-5 mins per side. Remove the salmon from the grill and rest for several mins before removing the skin and shredding it with a fork.
2. Mix all of the dressing ingredients in a small bowl until smooth. After adjusting the seasoning, refrigerate until service.
3. Mix the red wine vinegar, olive oil, oregano, dill, and salt & pepper in a medium bowl with a whisk. Then add Cucumber, cherry tomatoes, and red onion. Toss to blend.
4. Place the romaine lettuce on a big platter or a serving bowl. Salmon is topped with the cucumber combina- tion, olives, feta, and lettuce. Serve with dressing on the side.

Nutrition Information:
Calories: 361kcal, Protein: 33g, Carbohydrates: 11g, Fats: 20g

---

ARUGULA & FENNEL SALAD WITH LEMON VINAIGRETTE

Total Servngs: 8
Difficulty: Easy
Preparation Time: 20 minutes
Cook Time: 00 minutes
Total Time: 20 minutes

Ingredients

- ¼ cup extra-virgin olive oil
- 2 tsp grated lemon zest
- ¼ cup lemon juice
- ¼ tsp salt
- ¼ tsp ground pepper
- 10 ounces baby arugula
- 2 sliced small fennel bulbs
- 2 oz. Parmesan cheese shaved

Directions

1. In a large bowl, combine oil, lemon zest, lemon juice, salt, and pepper. Add arugula and fennel and toss together gently. If preferred, garnish with Parmesan and fennel fronds.

Nutrition Information:
Calories: 116kcal, Protein: 4g, Carbohydrates: 6g, Fats: 9g

Total Servings: 4
Difficulty: Easy
Preparation Time: 5 minutes
Cook Time: 12 minutes
Total Time: 17 minutes

TURKEY TACO LETTUCE WRAPS

Ingredients

- 1 tbsp olive oil
- 3/4 cup chopped yellow onion
- 1 lb 95% lean ground turkey
- 2 cloves garlic
- Salt and freshly ground black pepper
- 1 tbsp chili powder
- 1 tsp ground cumin
- ½ tsp paprika
- ½ cup tomato sauce
- ½ cup low-sodium chicken broth

Directions

1. On moderate-high heat, heat the olive oil in a non-stick pan. Add onion and saute for 2 mins. Add the turkey and garlic, season with salt and pepper, and cook, tossing and breaking up the turkey now and then, for about 5 mins or until the turkey is cooked all the way through.
2. Mix in chili powder, cumin, paprika, tomato sauce, and chicken broth. Reduce stove heat to low and cook for 5 mins or until the sauce has thickened. Serve the mixture on lettuce leaves with any toppings you want.

Nutrition Information:
Calories: 240kcal, Protein: 23g, Carbohydrates: 7g, Fats: 13g

---

Total Servings: 4
Difficulty: Medium
Preparation Time: 10 minutes
Cook Time: 10 minutes
Total Time: 20 minutes

CHICKEN CELERY SALAD

Ingredients

- 2 cups cooked shredded chicken (approx. 12 oz)
- 1 stalk chopped celery finely chopped
- ¼ cup diced onion
- ½ cup mayo
- 1 tsp dijon mustard
- ¼ tsp lemon zest
- 1 tsp chopped parsley
- ¼ tsp chopped dill
- ¼ tsp salt
- ¼ tsp black pepper
- Pinch paprika
- Garnish with more fresh parsley

Directions

1. Mix the chicken, chopped celery, and onion in a large bowl (leaving out the paprika). Add the mayonnaise, mustard, and zest from the lemon, herbs, and spices. Mix well by tossing.
2. Add a pinch of paprika on top and fresher parsley for decoration. Serve!

Nutrition Information:
Calories: 330kcal, Protein: 18g, Carbohydrates: 2g, Fats: 27g

Total Servngs: 6
Difficulty: Easy
Preparation Time: 15 minutes
Cook Time: 15 minutes
Total Time: 30 minutes

SPINACH SALAD

Ingredients

- ¼ cup red wine vinegar
- 2 tbsp powdered Swerve
- Salt and pepper
- ½ sliced red onion

Salad
- 5 oz. baby spinach
- 4 oz. strawberries, hulled and quartered
- ½ cup toasted pecans
- 4 oz. goat cheese crumbled

Directions

1. In a small pot, combine the vinegar, 1/4 cup water, sweetener, salt, and pepper. About 5 mins of heating over medium heat until the sweetness has dissolved.
2. In a bowl, place the onion and pour the vinegar mixture over it. Permit to rest for thirty minutes.
3. Combine Spinach, strawberries, pecans, and goat cheese in a big bowl. Drain and add the onions to the bowl. Toss the salad with the dressing and serve right away

Nutrition Information:
Calories: 123kcal, Protein: 5.3g, Carbohydrates: 4g, Fats: 10g

Total Servings: 4
Difficulty: Easy
Preparation Time: 15 minutes
Cook Time: 10 minutes
Total Time: 25 minutes

ASPARAGUS AND SPINACH SALAD WITH EGG

Ingredients

- 12 asparagus, average size
- 2 eggs size large, boiled and quartered
- 8 cups baby Spinach
- ¼ cup extra virgin olive oil
- 2 tbsp   lemon juice, freshly squeezed
- 1minced clove garlic
- Salt and ground pepper to taste

Directions

1. Prepare the asparagus in a pot of salted boiling water for about 10 mins. Make sure they are cooked to a firm bite.
2. Take the asparagus out of the pot with tongs or a slotted spoon since the spears are too fragile to go straight into a colander to drain. Rinse the asparagus in cold water to stop the cooking and
3. Get a salad bowl and put the Spinach in it. Mix the oil, lemon juice, minced garlic, salt, and pepper in a small bowl. With a fork, mix well until the vinaigrette is smooth. Pour the vinaigrette over the Spinach and stir it together.
4. Put the Spinach on each plate. Place the asparagus and boiled eggs cut into quarters on the Spinach and serve

Nutrition Information:
Calories: 190kcal, Protein: 5.3g, Carbohydrates: 4g, Fats: 18g

Total Servings: 4
Difficulty: Easy
Preparation Time: 25 minutes
Cook Time: 00 minutes
Total Time: 25 minutes

MEAL-PREP TURKEY COBB SALAD

Ingredients

- 3 tbsp red wine vinegar
- 3 tbsp extra-virgin olive oil
- 2 tsp Dijon mustard
- ¼ tsp salt
- ¼ tsp ground pepper
- 8 cups chopped romaine lettuce
- 2 scallions, sliced
- 1 cup halved cherry tomatoes
- 1 cup halved and sliced Cucumber
- 3 oz. cubed deli turkey
- 2 slices cooked bacon, halved
- 2 large hard-boiled eggs, halved
- ½ cup shredded sharp Cheddar cheese
- 1 avocado, pitted and quartered

Directions

1. Whisk vinegar, oil, mustard, salt, and pepper in a small bowl. Pour the dressing into four small glass jars.
2. Divide the romaine, scallions, tomatoes, Cucumber, turkey, bacon, egg halves, and Cheddar between four 3-cup-capable glass containers with lids.
3. Add avocado (if using) and dressing to the salad before serving and toss to coat.

Nutrition Information:
: Calories: 275kcal, Protein: 14g, Carbohydrates: 6g, Fats: 20g

---

Total Servings: 4
Difficulty: Easy
Preparation Time: 20 minutes
Cook Time: 00 minutes
Total Time: 20 minutes

GUACAMOLE CHOPPED SALAD

Ingredients

- 2 tbsp avocado oil
- 2 tbsp lime juice
- 1 grated clove garlic
- ¼ tsp salt
- ¼ tsp ground pepper
- 4 cups chopped romaine lettuce
- 2 diced ripe avocados
- 1 cup grape tomatoes, quartered
- ¼ cup slivered red onion
- 1 tbsp chopped pickled jalapeño pepper

Directions

1. In a large bowl, combine the olive oil, lime juice, garlic, and seasonings with salt and pepper. Toss the ro- maine, avocado, tomatoes, onion, and jalapenos gently with the dressing.

Nutrition Information:
Calories: 245kcal, Protein: 4g, Carbohydrates: 13g, Fats: 20g

Total Servngs: 6
Difficulty: Easy
Preparation Time: 10 minutes
Cook Time: 15 minutes
Total Time: 25 minutes

LOADED BROCCOLI SALAD

Ingredients

- 3 slices bacon
- ¼ cup sour cream
- ¼ cup mayonnaise
- 4 tsp rice vinegar or cider vinegar
- ¼ tsp ground pepper
- 4 cups chopped broccoli florets
- ½ cup sliced scallions
- ½ cup shredded extra-sharp Cheddar cheese

Directions

1. Cook bacon in a large stainless steel skillet over medium heat for 5-7 mins or until crisp. Transfer to a plate lined with paper towels. Save 1 tsp of bacon fat. When the bacon is cold enough to handle, chop it.
2. In a large bowl, combine sour cream, mayonnaise, vinegar, pepper, and the saved bacon fat. Add the broc- coli, scallions, cheese, and bacon. To coat with the dressing, mix well.

Nutrition Information:
Calories: 191kcal, Protein: 6g, Carbohydrates: 4g, Fats: 17

Total Servings: 6
Difficulty: Easy
Preparation Time: 15 minutes
Cook Time: 00 minutes
Total Time: 15 minutes

AVOCADO TUNA SALAD

Ingredients

- 3 tbsp extra-virgin olive oil
- 2 tbsp lemon juice
- ¼ tsp salt
- 2 medium chopped avocados
- 2 (5 oz.) cans of solid white tuna in oil, drained and flaked
- 4 cups romaine hearts
- 1 cup chopped English cucumber
- ⅓ cup crumbled feta cheese
- ¼ cup toasted sliced almonds
- ¼ cup chopped pitted Kalamata olives
- 3 tbsp chopped fresh flat-leaf parsley

Directions

1. Mix the oil, lemon juice, and salt in a large bowl. Add the avocados and toss gently to coat them well. Add tuna, romaine, Cucumber, feta, almonds, olives, and parsley to the avocado mixture, then gently mix them. Serve or put in the fridge for up to an hour.

Nutrition Information:
Calories: 338kcal, Protein: 17g, Carbohydrates: 10g, Fats: 27g

MIXED VEGETABLE SALAD WITH LIME DRESSING

Total Servings: 6
Difficulty: Easy
Preparation Time: 30 minutes
Cook Time: 00 minutes
Total Time: 30 minutes

Ingredients

- ¼ cup canola oil
- ¼ cup extra-virgin olive oil
- 3 tbsp lime juice
- 1 ½ tbsp finely chopped fresh cilantro
- ½ tsp salt
- ½ tsp ground pepper
- 2 cups mixed vegetables (steamed: sliced small red potatoes, carrots or beets, green beans, peas; raw: sliced radishes, cucumbers or tomatoes)
- 6 leaf lettuce
- 1 small bunch of watercress, large stems removed
- 1 large hard-boiled egg, sliced
- 1 slice of red onion broken into rings
- Crumbled Mexican queso fresco, feta for garnish

Directions

1. Whisk together the canola, olive oils, lime juice, cilantro, salt, and pepper in a medium bowl until fully com- bined. Toss in the mixed vegetables to coat them.
2. Lay lettuce on a large serving plate. Place the seasoned veggies on the serving platter. If desired, surround with watercress and top with egg, onion, and cheese.

Nutrition Information:
Calories: 214kcal, Protein: 3g, Carbohydrates: 7g, Fats: 19g

KALE & STRAWBERRY SALAD

Total Servings: 4
Difficulty: Easy
Preparation Time: 15 minutes
Cook Time: 00 minutes
Total Time: 15 minutes

Ingredients

- 8 cups chopped lacinato kale
- 5 tbsp extra-virgin olive oil, divided
- ½ tsp salt, divided
- 1 tbsp cider vinegar
- 1 tsp Dijon mustard
- ¼ tsp ground pepper
- 1 ½ cups hulled and halved fresh strawberries
- 2 oz. garlic-and-herb goat cheese, crumbled
- ⅛ cup chopped toasted walnuts

Directions

1. Mix the kale, 2 tbsp of oil, and 1/4 tsp salt in a large bowl. Massage the kale with your hands for about 1 min or until it is well coated.
2. Mix the vinegar, mustard, pepper, and the last 1/4 tsp of salt in a small bowl. Pour the last 3 tbsp of oil in slowly while constantly whisking.
3. Add strawberries, goat cheese, and walnuts to the kale. Drizzle the dressing over the salad and gently toss to mix.

Nutrition Information:
Calories: 301kcal, Protein: 6g, Carbohydrates: 9g, Fats: 27g

Total Servngs: 8
Difficulty: Easy
Preparation Time: 30 minutes
Cook Time: 00 minutes
Total Time: 30 minutes

EAT-THE- RAINBOW CHOPPED SALAD

Ingredients

- ¼ cup white balsamic vinegar
- ¼ cup extra-virgin olive oil
- ½ tsp salt
- ¼ tsp ground pepper
- 2 diced large carrots, diced
- 1 diced large yellow bell pepper
- 2 cups chopped kale
- 1 ¼ cups chopped red cabbage
- 1 cup quartered grape tomatoes
- 1 cup mozzarella pearls
- ½ cup thinly sliced fresh basil
- 2 sliced scallions

Directions

1. Whisk together the vinegar, oil, salt, and pepper in a large bowl. Add carrots, bell pepper, kale, cabbage, tomatoes, mozzarella, basil, and scallions. Toss to coat.

Nutrition Information:
Calories: 140kcal, Protein: 5g, Carbohydrates: 7g, Fats: 10g

Total Servings: 4
Difficulty: Easy
Preparation Time: 20 minutes
Cook Time: 00 minutes
Total Time: 20 minutes

SHRIMP COBB SALAD WITH DIJON DRESSING

Ingredients

- 3 tbsp extra-virgin olive oil
- 3 tbsp white wine vinegar
- 2 tbsp finely chopped shallot
- 1 tbsp Dijon mustard
- ½ tsp ground pepper
- ¼ tsp salt
- 10 cups mixed greens
- 12 cooked extra-large shrimp, peeled and halved lengthwise
- 1 cup halved cherry tomatoes
- 1 cup Persian cucumber chunks
- 2 large hard-boiled eggs, peeled and halved
- 1 avocado, diced
- 2 slices cooked bacon, crumbled
- ¼ cup crumbled blue cheese

Directions

1. In a jar with a cover, combine oil, vinegar, shallot, mustard, pepper, and salt. Shake until well blended.
2. Plate salad greens in a mound. Drizzle half the dressing over the salad and toss to coat. Arrange shrimp, tomatoes, cucumbers, egg halves, avocado, bacon, and blue cheese on top in a decorative manner. Drizzle the remaining dressing over the salad.

Nutrition Information:
Calories: 378kcal, Protein: 29g, Carbohydrates: 12g, Fats: 25g

Total Servings: 2
Difficulty: Easy
Preparation Time: 10 minutes
Cook Time: 25 minutes
Total Time: 35 minutes

SPICED GRILLED TURKEY WITH CAULIFLOWER TABBOULEH

Ingredients

- 5 tbsp extra-virgin olive oil, divided
- 2 ½ tsp ground cumin, divided
- 1 ½ tsp dried marjoram
- ¾ tsp salt, divided
- ¼ tsp ground allspice
- ¼ tsp cayenne pepper
- 1 pound boneless, skinless turkey breast, trimmed
- ¼ cup lemon juice
- 2 cups fresh riced cauliflower
- 2 cups flat-leaf parsley leaves
- 1 cup diced Cucumber
- 1 cup halved cherry tomatoes
- ¼ cup sliced scallions

Directions

1. Gets the grill going on medium-high heat. Mix 2 tbsp of oil, 2 tsp each of cumin, marjoram, 1/2 tsp of salt, allspice, and cayenne in a small bowl. Brush the turkey.
2. Grill the turkey, turning it now and then, for 10-12 mins.
3. In the meantime, mix the lemon juice, 1/2 tsp of cumin, 1/4 tsp of salt, and the remaining 3 tbsp of oil in a large bowl. Mix the cauliflower rice, parsley, Cucumber, tomatoes, and scallions.
4. Place the turkey on a clean cutting board and rest for 5 mins. Cut it into thin slices and put them on top of the tabbouleh.

Nutrition Information:
Calories: 341kcal, Protein: 28g, Carbohydrates: 8g, Fats: 21g

---

Total Servings: 4
Difficulty: Medium
Preparation Time: 15 minutes
Cook Time: 00 minutes
Total Time: 15 minutes

SUMMER SHRIMP SALAD

Ingredients

- 1 ¼ pounds raw shrimp, peeled and deveined
- ¼ cup extra-virgin olive oil
- 10 sprigs of fresh thyme
- 4 crushed cloves of garlic
- ¼ tsp salt
- ¼ tsp ground pepper
- ¼ cup lemon juice
- 1 diced medium English cucumber
- 3 chopped large heirloom tomatoes
- ½ cup chopped fresh basil, plus extra for garnish

Directions

1. Preheat oven to 350F. Put shrimp, oil, thyme, and garlic on a baking sheet with a rim. Put salt and pepper on it. Bake for 8-10 mins, or until the shrimps are pink and firm.
2. Put the shrimp into a big bowl (discard thyme and garlic). Stir in the lemon juice to coat. Mix cucumber, tomatoes, and basil in with a spoon. Put the shrimp and vegetables in a bowl to be served. Serve with any dressing left in the bowl and more basil if you want.

Nutrition Information:
Calories: 290kcal, Protein: 30g, Carbohydrates: 10g, Fats: 15g

CHICKEN BACON AVOCADO SALAD WITH ASPARAGUS

Total Servings: 4
Difficulty: Easy
Preparation Time: 15 minutes
Cook Time: 15 minutes
Total Time: 30 minutes

Ingredients

- 8 slices good quality thick bacon (smoked)
- 1 tbsp butter
- 2 cups chopped asparagus
- 1 tsp lemon pepper seasoning (more to taste)
- 4 cups spinach, cut or torn into bite-sized pieces
- 8 oz. chicken breast slices
- 1 large ripe avocado
- ¼ cup good quality olive oil
- ¼ cup good quality balsamic vinegar
- fresh basil for topping

Directions

1. Cook bacon according to the instructions on the package (I go for crispy on this one). Drain on a platter lined with paper towels and break or chop into bite-sized pieces.
2. In a small stainless steel skillet, melt the butter over high heat. Add the asparagus, sprinkle with lemon pep- per, and cook until golden brown and roasted in appearance. I enjoy the small charred bits, so I cooked it a little longer. Depending on your preference, you may cook asparagus for as long as you like.
3. The chicken has been cut into bite-sized pieces. The Spinach, chicken, asparagus, and bacon are layered. Slice the avocado and scoop out the flesh with a spoon; arrange it on top of the salad. Drizzle or toss the olive oil and balsamic vinegar over the salad. Add fresh basil, salt, and pepper to taste.

Nutrition Information:
Calories: 391kcal, Protein: 20.2g, Carbohydrates: 11g, Fats: 30g

SALMON CAESAR SALAD

Total Servings: 4
Difficulty: Medium
Preparation Time: 20 minutes
Cook Time: 00 minutes
Total Time: 20 minutes

Ingredients

- 1 ½ tbsp extra-virgin olive oil
- 4 (5 oz) skinless salmon fillets
- 1 tsp ground pepper, divided
- ⅛ tsp salt plus ½ tsp, divided
- ½ cup buttermilk
- ¼ cup nonfat plain Greek yogurt
- ¼ cup grated Parmigiano-Reggiano cheese
- 2 tbsp lemon juice
- 1 ½ tsp Worcestershire sauce
- 1 tsp grated garlic
- ½ tsp Dijon mustard
- 5 cups chopped romaine lettuce
- 3 cups chopped radicchio
- 3 tbsp thinly sliced fresh basil, plus more for garnish
- 1 ½ tbsp chopped fresh tarragon

Directions

1. In a large skillet that doesn't stick, heats the oil over medium-high heat until it shimmers. Put 1/2 tsp of pepper and 1/8 tsp of salt on the salmon. Add salmon to the pan and cook for 3-4 mins per side or until it is golden brown and flakes easily with a fork. Place on a plate and break up into big pieces.
2. Mix the buttermilk, yogurt, cheese, lemon juice, Worcestershire sauce, garlic, mustard, and the last 1/2 tsp of pepper and salt in a large bowl. In a small bowl, set aside 1/4 cup of the dressing. Put the lettuce, radicchio, basil, and tarragon in the large bowl and toss to coat.
3. Put the salad on a plate and put the salmon on top. Serve with 1/4 cup of dressing that is reserved and more basil, if you want.

Nutrition Information:
Calories: 291kcal, Protein: 34g, Carbohydrates: 7g, Fats: 12g

Total Servings: 8
Difficulty: Medium
Preparation Time: 20 minutes
Cook Time: 00 minutes
Total Time: 20 minutes

APPLE & CHEDDAR SIDE SALAD WITH MUSTARD VINAIGRETTE

Ingredients

- 1 tbsp chopped shallot
- 1 tbsp whole-grain mustard
- 2 tbsp cider vinegar
- ¼ tsp ground pepper
- Salt to taste
- ¼ cup extra-virgin olive oil
- 8 cups mixed salad greens, like arugula, Spinach, and green leaf lettuce
- 1 cup sliced celery
- 1 large chopped red apple
- ½ cup shaved extra-sharp Cheddar cheese
- ½ cup toasted chopped pecans

Directions

1. In a large bowl, combine shallot, mustard, vinegar, pepper, and salt (or small bowl, if making ahead). Whisk oil until thoroughly mixed.
2. Add the greens, celery, apple, cheese, and pecans before serving. Toss the dressing with the greens until they are evenly coated.

Nutrition Information:
Calories: 180kcal, Protein: 3.3g, Carbohydrates: 6.8g, Fats: 15g

---

Total Servings: 4
Difficulty: Medium
Preparation Time: 15 minutes
Cook Time: 00 minutes
Total Time: 15 minutes

SPINACH & ARTICHOKE SALAD WITH PARMESAN VINAIGRETTE

Ingredients

- 1 (15 oz) can of quarter artichoke hearts
- 1 recipe Parmesan Vinaigrette
- 1 (5 oz) package of baby spinach
- 6 hard-boiled eggs
- ¼ cup chopped unsalted pistachios

Directions

1. Use paper towels or a clean dish towel to line a sheet pan. Drain the artichokes in a strainer with wire mesh and give them a good rinse under cold water. Drain them again. Set the artichokes in a single layer on the pan you just made (to get rid of excess water), and set them aside.
2. Put 2 tbsp of vinaigrette in each of the 4 small containers with lids.
3. Split the artichokes between 4 containers that each hold one serving. On top of each one, put a quarter of the Spinach. Close the lids and put the containers in the fridge for up to 4 days.
4. Slice up 1 1/2 hard-boiled eggs and put them in the meal-prep container. Before serving, dress the salad with the vinaigrette and sprinkle with 1 tbsp of pistachios.

Nutrition Information:
Calories: 324kcal, Protein: 16g, Carbohydrates: 11g, Fats: 23g

Total Servngs: 6
Difficulty: Easy
Preparation Time: 20 minutes
Cook Time: 00 minutes
Total Time: 20 minutes

VEGAN CREAMY COLESLAW

Ingredients

- 6 tbsp vegan or eggless mayonnaise
- 1 tbsp Dijon mustard
- 1 tbsp cider vinegar
- 1 tsp sugar
- ½ tsp caraway seeds or celery seed
- Pinch of salt
- Pinch of ground pepper
- 2 cups thinly sliced red cabbage
- 2 cups thinly sliced green cabbage
- 1 cup shredded carrots (2 medium)

Directions

1. Combine mayonnaise, mustard, vinegar, and sugar in a large bowl. Add pepper, salt, and caraway seeds (or celery seeds). Mix in red cabbage, green cabbage, and carrots.

Nutrition Information:
Calories: 115kcal, Protein: 0.8g, Carbohydrates: 5.7g, Fats: 10g

Total Servings: 5
Difficulty: Easy
Preparation Time: 20 minutes
Cook Time: 00 minutes
Total Time: 20 minutes

AVOCADO RANCH CHICKEN SALAD

Ingredients

- 1 ripe avocado, halved and pitted
- ⅓ cup ranch dressing
- 2 tbsp chopped pickled jalapeño
- 1 tbsp white wine vinegar
- ¼ tsp salt
- ¼ tsp ground pepper
- 3 cups shredded cooked chicken
- ½ cup diced celery
- ¼ cup diced red onion

Directions

1. Scoop avocado into a blender. Add ranch dressing, vinegar, pickled jalapeño, salt & pepper. Blend until it's smooth. Move to a medium-sized bowl. Mix the chicken, celery, and red onion using a rubber spatula. Serve at room temperature or put in the fridge for about 2 hours until it's cold.

Nutrition Information:
Calories: 361kcal, Protein: 32g, Carbohydrates: 4g, Fats: 23g

Total Servings: 5
Difficulty: Medium
Preparation Time: 10 minutes
Cook Time: 20 minutes
Total Time: 30 minutes

ROASTED MUSHROOM SALAD WITH SHERRY DRESSING

Ingredients

- 1 pound mixed mushrooms
- 1 small onion, halved and sliced
- 3 tbsp extra-virgin olive oil, divided
- ¼ tsp salt, divided
- 2 tbsp lemon juice
- 1 ½ tsp chopped fresh thyme
- ¼ tsp ground pepper
- 3 tbsp dry sherry
- 2 minced cloves garlic
- 8 cups bitter salad greens, such as frisée or arugula
- 2 tbsp shaved Parmesan cheese

Directions

1. Turn oven on to 450°F. Mix the mushrooms, onion, 1 tbsp of oil, and 1/8 tsp salt in a large bowl. Spread even- ly on a large baking sheet with a rim. 15-20 mins, stirring now and then, until soft and golden brown.
2. In the large bowl, mix the last 2 tbsp of oil, the lemon juice, the thyme, 1/8 tsp of salt, and the pepper.
3. Take the mushrooms and sauce out of the oven. Add the sherry and garlic to the pan right away. Whisk
4. and scrape up any bits that have been browned. Then add the mixture to the dressing in the bowl. Add the greens and stir to coat them. Serve the salad with Parmesan cheese on top.

Nutrition Information:
Calories: 107kcal, Protein: 4g, Carbohydrates: 6g, Fats: 8g

Total Servings: 4
Difficulty: Medium
Preparation Time: 25 minutes
Cook Time: 30 minutes
Total Time: 55 minutes

TOFU CUCUMBER SALAD WITH SPICY PEANUT DRESSING

Ingredients

- Peanut Dressing
- 1 ½ tbsp natural peanut butter
- 1 tbsp reduced-sodium soy sauce
- 1 tbsp rice vinegar
- 1 ½ tsp toasted (dark) sesame oil
- 1 tsp black bean-garlic sauce
- 1 tsp minced fresh ginger
- ½ tsp chile-garlic sauce
- ½ tsp sugar
- ¼ tsp finely chopped garlic
- ¼ tsp ground Sichuan peppercorns

Salad
- 8 oz extra-firm water-packed tofu, drained and cut into 1/2-inch cubes
- 1 large English cucumber, quartered and sliced
- 1 cup coarsely chopped cilantro, divided
- ¼ cup chopped salted roasted peanuts
- ¼ cup thinly sliced scallion greens

Directions

1. Blend peanut butter, soy sauce, vinegar, sesame oil, black bean-garlic sauce, ginger, chile-garlic sauce, sug- ar, garlic, and crushed peppercorns in a medium bowl to produce the dressing.
2. To make a salad, combine tofu, Cucumber, and three-quarters of a cup of cilantro in a large bowl. Then add 2 tbsp of the dressing and mix until the salad is evenly coated. Cover and refrigerate for 30 mins.
3. Transfer salad to a serving bowl to serve. Drizzle the remaining dressing over the salad. To finish, garnish with peanuts, scallions, and leftover

Nutrition Information:
Calories: 167kcal, Protein: 10g, Carbohydrates: 7g, Fats: 11g

VEGGIE EGG SALAD

Total Servngs: 4
Difficulty: Easy
Preparation Time: 25 minutes
Cook Time: 00 minutes
Total Time: 25 minutes

Ingredients

- 3 tbsp nonfat plain yogurt
- 3 tbsp reduced-fat mayonnaise
- ¼ tsp freshly ground pepper
- ⅛ tsp salt
- 8 hard-boiled eggs
- ½ cup finely chopped carrot
- ½ cup chopped Cucumber, peeled and seeded if desired
- ¼ cup sliced scallions

Directions

1. Mix the yogurt, mayonnaise, pepper, and salt in a medium bowl.
2. Cut eggs in half and throw away 4 of the yolks (or save them for another use). Add the whites and the other 4 yolks to the bowl and mash until the consistency you want is reached. Mix in the carrot, Cucumber, and scallions gently.

Nutrition Information:
Calories: 135kcal, Protein: 11g, Carbohydrates: 6g, Fats: 7g

CRUNCHY CONFETTI TUNA SALAD

Total Servings: 4
Difficulty: Madium
Preparation Time: 25 minutes
Cook Time: 00 minutes
Total Time: 25 minutes

Ingredients

- Dressing
- ¼ cup nonfat plain Greek yogurt
- ¼ cup low-fat mayonnaise
- 1 tbsp whole-grain mustard
- 1 tsp lemon juice
- 1 tsp chopped fresh dill
- ¼ tsp kosher salt
- Ground pepper to taste
- Salad
- 2 5-ounce cans of chunk light tuna packed in olive oil, drained
- 1 small carrot, diced small
- 2 stalks celery, diced small
- ¼ cup coarsely chopped celery leaves
- ¼ cup shredded radishes
- ¼ cup diced yellow bell pepper
- 2 tbsp minced red onion
- 1 scallion, thinly sliced
- 8 large Bibb lettuce leaves

Directions

1. Mix yogurt, mayonnaise, mustard, lemon juice, dill, salt, and pepper in a medium bowl.
2. To prepare a salad, place tuna in a bowl and, using a fork, break it into small pieces. Add carrot, celery, cel- ery leaves (or parsley), radishes, red bell pepper, onion, and scallion to the dish. Stir with care to mix.
3. To serve, place two lettuce leaves atop each other. Distribute the salad between the lettuce leaves.

Nutrition Information:
Calories: 135kcal, Protein: 11g, Carbohydrates: 6g, Fats: 7g

Total Servings: 6
Difficulty: Medium
Preparation Time: 20 minutes
Cook Time: 00 minutes
Total Time: 20 minutes

CRAB SALAD

Ingredients

- ⅓ cup whole-milk plain strained Greek yogurt
- ¼ cup mayonnaise
- 2 tbsp chopped fresh dill, plus extra for garnish
- 2 tbsp coarsely chopped fresh parsley
- 1 tsp grated lemon zest, plus more for garnish
- 3 tbsp lemon juice
- 1 tsp 30%-less-sodium Old Bay seasoning
- 1 pound lump crabmeat, drained and picked over
- 1 sliced small red bell pepper
- 2 sliced medium celery stalks
- ½ cup very thinly sliced red onion
- 6 cups chopped romaine heart

Directions

1. In a medium bowl, stir together the yogurt, mayonnaise, dill, parsley, lemon zest, lemon juice, and Old Bay until everything is mixed together.
2. Mix in the crab, bell pepper, onion, and celery. Serve the crab salad on a bed of lettuce. You can add more lemon zest and dill for decoration if you want.

Nutrition Information:
Calories: 185kcal, Protein: 20g, Carbohydrates: 5g, Fats: 9g

Total Servings: 2
Difficulty: Medium
Preparation Time: 10 minutes
Cook Time: 5 minutes
Total Time: 15 minutes

TUNA NICOISE SALAD

Ingredients

- 8 oz. tuna steak
- 2 egg
- 2 oz. baby spinach
- 2 oz. green beans
- 3 oz. broccoli
- 2 oz. cucumber
- 2 radish
- ¼ cup black olives
- ½ cup chopped parsley
- 2 tsp olive oil
- 2 tsp balsamic vinegar
- 1 tsp Dijon mustard
- 1 tsp pepper

Directions

1. Boil the egg, and then let it cool. Steam broccoli and beans then set aside. 2-3 mins in the microwave with a little water do the trick.
2. Put a little oil in a pan and turn the heat up high. Put pepper on all sides of the tuna, then put it in a pan and cook for about 2 mins on each side.
3. Put the Spinach in your bowl or plate of salad. Cut up the Cucumber and egg, so they are easy to eat. On top of the Spinach, add.
4. Slice up the radish and mix it with the broccoli, beans, and olives. Add to the salad of Spinach. The tuna is cut up and added to the salad.
5. Mix the olive oil, balsamic vinegar, mustard, salt, and pepper in a bowl with a whisk.
6. Chop up the parsley and add it to the vinaigrette. You can pour the vinaigrette over the salad with a spoon.

Nutrition Information:
Calories: 376cal, Protein: 39g, Carbohydrates: 10g, Fats: 20g

FISH RECIPES

Total Servings: 4
Difficulty: Easy
Preparation Time: 5 minutes
Cook Time: 20 minutes
Total Time: 25 minutes

SHRIMP SCAMPI WITH ZUCCHINI NOODLES

Ingredients

- Shrimp:
- 2 tbsp. olive oil
- 1 lb. large shrimp, peeled and deveined
- Salt and crushed black pepper
- Sauce:
- 1 tbsp. olive oil
- 2 tbsp. minced garlic
- 1 medium shallot, minced
- ¼ cup chicken broth
- ¼ cup softened butter
- 2 tbsp. lemon juice
- Salt and crushed black pepper
- Assembly:
- 1 lb. fresh zucchini, spiralized
- 4 tbsp. chopped parsley

Directions

1. Toss zucchini noodles with 2 tsp salt and set aside for 20 mins. Meanwhile, prepare shrimp, add oil to the non-stick frying pan, and sauté shrimp for 4-5 mins (stirring and flipping shrimp continuously).
2. Powder salt and pepper as per your taste and sauté more for 1 minute. Remove shrimp and set it aside (but keep warm). Add oil to the same non-stick pan, cook minced garlic with shallot and cook for 2-3 mins. Add broth, butter, lemon juice, salt, and pepper to the pan.
3. Cook for 4-5 mins stir during cooking (scrape down the sides with the spatula). Rinse noodles under runny water to remove the salt and salty water from the noodles. Add noodles to the pan and cook for 2-3 mins, then add shrimp to the pan, stir and sauté for 1-2 mins. Serve and enjoy.

Nutrition Information:
Calories: 348kcal, Protein: 26g, Carbohydrate: 7g, Fat: 24g

Total Servings: 4
Difficulty: Easy
Preparation Time: 5 minutes
Cook Time: 20 minutes
Total Time: 25 minutes

SHRIMP COCONUT CURRY

Ingredients

- 16 oz. shrimp, peeled and deveined
- 1 tbsp. coconut oil
- 1 cup coconut milk
- ½ tsp. minced ginger
- 1 tsp. curry powder
- ½ cup chopped onion
- ½ tbsp. minced garlic
- ½ tsp. cinnamon powder
- ¼ tsp. ground cumin
- Salt and crushed black pepper

Directions

1. Toss shrimp in a bowl with salt and pepper (about ½ tsp each), then cover the bowl and set aside for later use. Put the non-stick pot over medium heat, add oil and cook ginger with chopped onion and garlic for 3-4 mins.
2. Add coconut milk, curry powder, cinnamon powder, and ground cumin. Take a boil, then simmer for 4-5 mins over medium-low heat. Add shrimp to the pot with the liquid (if any).
3. Cook for 10-12 mins. Remove shrimp curry from heat, serve it with cauliflower rice and enjoy.

Nutrition Information:
Calories: 347kcal, Protein: 28g, Carbohydrate: 7g, Fat: 23g

Total Servngs: 1
Difficulty: Easy
Preparation Time: 10 minutes
Cook Time: 10 minutes
Total Time: 20 minutes

SHRIMP FRIED RICE

Ingredients

- 1 tbsp. sesame oil divided
- 100g raw shrimp, tails and shells removed
- 1 small egg
- 2 tbsp. small onion, diced
- 1 tsp minced garlic
- ½ tsp minced ginger
- ¼ cup frozen peas and carrots
- ½ cup cauliflower rice
- ½ tbsp soy sauce
- ½ tbsp oyster sauce
- ½ tbsp chopped green onions

Directions

1. In a large non-stick deep bottom skillet, heat ½ of the sesame oil over medium heat. Cook until the shrimp is done completely. Take it out of the pan and put it in a warm place.
2. Coat the wok with non-stick spray. Add and scramble the egg over medium heat, then move them to a plate to keep warm. Add the onion to the wok and stir it around. Cook for about 3–5 minutes or until the onions
3. are soft. Take from the wok and set it aside.
4. Stir-fry the garlic and ginger for 30 seconds in the wok with leftover sesame oil. Stir fry for 2 more minutes after adding the frozen peas and carrots. Add the cauliflower rice and mix everything. Put the oyster sauce and soy sauce in the pan. Stir to heat everything.
5. Put the onions, eggs, and shrimp back in the wok, and stir in the green onions. Warm up and serve right away. Enjoy!

Nutrition Information:
Calories: 341kcal, Protein: 30g, Carbohydrates: 8g, Fats, 21g

Total Servings: 4
Difficulty: Medium
Preparation Time: 15 minutes
Cook Time: 00 minutes
Total Time: 15 minutes

GRILLED LOBSTER TAIL

Ingredients

- 4 lobster tails
- 1 tbsp. olive oil
- Salt and crushed black pepper
- ¼ cup melted butter
- 1 tbsp. minced garlic
- 1 tbsp. lemon juice
- ½ tsp smoked paprika
- Pinch cayenne pepper

Directions

1. Burn your outdoor grill (having cover/lid) for 15 mins. In a small bowl, add melted butter and mix it with minced garlic, lemon juice, smoked paprika powder, and a pinch of cayenne pepper. Beat them well and set them aside for later use.
2. Cut the lobster tail lengthwise (start from the opposite of the bottom shell). Not to cut all and deep. Brush olive oil over the lobster tails and powder salt & pepper over the lobster.
3. Put the lobster tails over the grill grates, cover the grill and cook for 3-4 mins. Now flip the tail and cook un- covered for 3-4 mins over medium-low heat. Baste the garlic butter sauce after every 1 minute. When done, drop the leftover sauce (if any) on top. Serve and enjoy.

Nutrition Information:
Calories: 336kcal, Protein: 38g, Carbohydrate: 1g, Fat: 18g

Total Servings: 4
Difficulty: Medium
Preparation Time: 5 minutes
Cook Time: 25 minutes
Total Time: 30 minutes

LOBSTER BISQUE

Ingredients

- 6 lb. lobster
- 4 cups water or more if needed
- 1½ cups coconut milk
- 3 tbsp. red curry paste
- 2 tbsp. lime juice
- Salt and crushed black pepper (if needed)

Directions

1. In the instant pot, add lobster with 2 cups, tight the lid and cook for 8-10 mins. Then remove the pot from heat and leave for 10 mins. Meanwhile, put the large stockpot over medium heat, add 2 cups water and take a boil.
2. Pour in coconut milk, red curry paste, and fresh lime juice, and cook for 10-15 mins until fragrant. Now crack the lobster shell and remove the meat (you get about 4 cups of cooked meat).
3. Add lobster meat to the stockpot and cook for 3-5 mins; add salt and pepper (as much as you like). Evenly divide into four bowls, garnish with chopped cilantro, serve and enjoy.

Nutrition Information:
Calories: 386kcal, Protein: 30g, Carbohydrate: 8g, Fat: 26g

Total Servings: 4
Difficulty: Easy
Preparation Time: 08 minutes
Cook Time: 07 minutes
Total Time: 15 minutes

AIR FRYER LOBSTER TAILS

Ingredients

- 4 lobster tails
- ½ cup softened butter
- 1 tbsp. lemon zest
- 1 tbsp. minced garlic
- Salt and crushed black pepper
- ½ tsp. smoked paprika
- 1 tbsp. chopped fresh parsley

Directions

1. Mix butter with lemon zest, minced garlic, smoked paprika, salt, and pepper in a bowl. Beat them well and set them aside to use later. Wash and pat dry the lobster tails.
2. Cut the lobster tail shell (just cut the shell; don't try to cut deep). Brush the lobster tail with butter sauce and place in the air fryer basket, and cook for 5-7 mins at 380F.
3. When done, remove from the basket and place on a large plate. Drop butter sauce on lobster tails, serve and enjoy.

Nutrition Information:
Calories: 400kcal, Protein: 38g, Carbohydrate: 2g, Fat: 25

Total Servngs: 4
Difficulty: Easy
Preparation Time: 5 minutes
Cook Time: 15 minutes
Total Time: 20 minutes

CRAB CAKES

Ingredients

- ½ cup seasoned breadcrumbs, divided
- 2 green onions, chopped
- ¼ cup chopped sweet red pepper
- 1 large egg, beaten
- ¼ cup low-fat mayonnaise
- 1 tbsp. lemon juice
- ½ tsp. garlic powder
- 500g canned crabmeat, drained, flaked, and without cartilage
- 2 tbsp. butter

Directions

1. Mix ¼ cup breadcrumbs, green onions, red pepper, egg, low-fat mayonnaise, lemon juice, garlic powder, and cayenne in a large bowl. Add in crab meat.
2. Put the breadcrumbs that are left in a shallow bowl. Make two-inch balls out of the crab mixture and divide them into eight pieces. Coat with breadcrumbs and shape into ½-inch thick patties.
3. Over medium-high heat, melt butter in a large skillet that doesn't stick. Add the crab cakes and cook on each side for 3–4 minutes until golden brown.

Nutrition Information:
Calories: 280kcal, Protein: 29g, Carbohydrate: 7g, Fat: 15g

Total Servings: 4
Difficulty: Easy
Preparation Time: 5 minutes
Cook Time: 15 minutes
Total Time: 20 minutes

RED PEPPER & PARMESAN TILAPIA

Ingredients

- 1 large egg, lightly beaten
- 1 tbsp olive oil
- ½ cup grated parmesan cheese
- 1 tsp. Italian seasoning
- 1 tsp. crushed red pepper flakes
- ½ tsp. crushed black pepper
- 4 tilapia fillets (6 oz each weight)

Directions

1. Turn the oven on to 425°. Put the egg in a wide bowl. Mix the cheese, Italian seasoning, pepper flakes, and pepper in another shallow bowl. Dip fillets in egg, then in a mixture of cheeses.
2. Place fillets into the 15x10x1-inch pan sprayed with cooking spray. Roast for 13-15 mins until you can pull the fish apart with a fork.

Nutrition Information:
Calories: 303kcal, Protein: 38g, Carbohydrate: 4g, Fat: 15g

Total Servings: 4
Difficulty: Easy
Preparation Time: 5 minutes
Cook Time: 10 minutes
Total Time: 15 minutes

TOMATO WALNUT TILAPIA

Ingredients

- 4 tilapia fillets (4 oz each weight)
- ¼ tsp. salt
- ¼ tsp. pepper
- 1 tbsp. butter
- 1 medium tomato, thinly sliced
- Topping:
- ½ cup soft breadcrumbs
- ¼ cup chopped walnuts
- 2 tbsp. lemon juice
- 1½ tsp. butter, melted

Directions

1. Add salt and pepper to the fillets. Fillets are cooked in butter over medium-high heat for about two to three minutes on each side in a large pan that has been sprayed with cooking spray. P
2. lace the fish fillet on the broiler pan and top it with the tomato. Mix the ingredients for the topping, then spoon it over the tomato slices.
3. Broil 3–4 inches from the heat until the topping is lightly browned and the fish flakes apart with a fork, about 2 minutes.

Nutrition Information:
Calories: 266kcal, Protein: 38g, Carbohydrate: 6g, Fat: 10g

CRUMB-COATED RED SNAPPER

Total Servings: 4
Difficulty: Easy
Preparation Time: 10 minutes
Cook Time: 5 minutes
Total Time: 15 minutes

Ingredients

- ½ cup dry breadcrumbs
- 2 tbsp. grated Parmesan cheese
- 1 tsp. lemon-pepper seasoning
- ¼ tsp. salt
- 4 red snapper fillets (6 oz each weight)
- 2 tbsp olive oil

Directions

1. Mix the breadcrumbs, cheese, lemon pepper, and salt in a shallow bowl. Add the fillets one at a time and turn them to coat them.
2. In batches, cook fillets in oil in a heavy skillet over medium heat for 4–5 minutes on each side or until the fish starts to flake apart with a fork.

Nutrition Information:
Calories: 250kcal, Protein: 38g, Carbohydrate: 10g, Fat: 10g

Total Servngs: 4
Difficulty: Easy
Preparation Time: 10 minutes
Cook Time: 15 minutes
Total Time: 25 minutes

BROILED GREEK FISH FILLETS

Ingredients

- ¼ cup chopped red onion
- ¼ cup plain yogurt
- 2 tbsp. melted butter
- 1 tbsp. lime juice
- 1 tsp. dill weed
- ½ tsp. paprika
- ¼ tsp. garlic powder
- 4 tilapia fillets (8 oz each weight)
- ¼ tsp. salt
- ¼ tsp. pepper
- ½ cup crumbled feta cheese
- ½ cup pitted and sliced Greek olives

Directions

1. Heat the broiler. Mix the first seven things. Put powder salt and pepper over the tilapia in a 15x10x1-inch pan. Spread the onion mixture down the middle of each fillet, and then add cheese and olives.
2. Broil 3–4 inches from the heat for 6–9 minutes or until the fish flakes apart with a fork.

Nutrition Information:
Calories: 336kcal, Protein: 42g, Carbohydrate: 6g, Fat: 16g

Total Servings: 4
Difficulty: Easy
Preparation Time: 5 minutes
Cook Time: 10 minutes
Total Time: 15 minutes

SKILLET SEA SCALLOPS

Ingredients

- ½ cup dry breadcrumbs
- ½ tsp. salt
- 1 lb. sea scallops
- 2 tbsp. butter
- 2 tbsp. olive oil
- ¼ cup white wine
- 2 tbsp. lemon juice
- ½ tbsp. minced garlic
- 1 tsp. minced fresh parsley

Directions

1. Mix salt with breadcrumbs in a shallow bowl. Coat both sides of the scallops with the crumb mixture by dipping them and patting them down.
2. Over moderate heat, melt the butter and oil in a large pan. Add the scallops and cook for 1½-2 minutes on each side until they are firm and clear. Remove from the heat, then from the pan, and set aside to keep warm.
3. Add the wine, lemon juice, and garlic to the same pan, and bring to a boil. Mix in some parsley. Drizzle over scallops and serve immediately.

Nutrition Information:
Calories: 267kcal, Protein: 23g, Carbohydrate: 10g, Fat: 15g

Total Servings: 4
Difficulty: Easy
Preparation Time: 10 minutes
Cook Time: 15 minutes
Total Time: 25 minutes

LEMONY PARSLEY BAKED COD

Ingredients

- 3 tbsp. chopped parsley
- 2 tbsp. lemon juice
- 1 tbsp. grated lemon zest
- 2 tbsp. olive oil
- 1 tbsp. minced garlic
- Salt and crushed black pepper
- 4 cod fillets (6 oz each weight)
- 2 green onions, chopped

Directions

1. Set your oven heat range to 400°F to preheat. Mix chopped parsley, lemon juice, lemon zest, olive oil, minced garlic, salt, and crushed black pepper in a bowl.
2. Put the cod in an 11x7-inch baking dish and sprinkle the parsley mixture on top. Spread chopped green on- ion on top. Cover and bake for 10-15 minutes, or until the fish flakes easily with a fork.

Nutrition Information:
Calories: 229kcal, Protein: 34g, Carbohydrate: 3g, Fat: 9g

Total Servings: 4
Difficulty: Easy
Preparation Time: 15 minutes
Cook Time: 15 minutes
Total Time: 30 minutes

GRILLED SALMON FILLETS WITH DILL SAUCE

Ingredients

- 2 medium lemons
- 4 salmon fillets (6 oz each weight)
- Lemon-Dill Sauce:
- 2½ tsp. cornstarch
- ½ cup water
- ¼ cup lemon juice
- 4 tsp. butter
- 3 lemon slices, quartered
- 1 tbsp. snipped fresh dill
- Salt and crushed black pepper
- Pinch of dried chervil

Directions

1. Cut the ends off each lemon and slice them into thick slices. Cover the salmon and lemon slices and grill them over high heat on an oiled grill rack for 7-10 minutes (flip after half-time).
2. You can also broil them 3–4 inches from the heat simultaneously. For the dill sauce, mix the cornstarch, wa- ter, snipped fresh dill, dried chervil and lemon juice in a small saucepan. Add the butter. Stir until the sauce thickens and bubbles (cook over medium heat).
3. Take it off the heat and stir the lemon slices cut into quarters and the spices. Serve the grilled salmon and lemon slices with dill sauce.

Nutrition Information:
Calories: 340kcal, Protein: 34g, Carbohydrate: 6g, Fat: 20g

Total Servngs: 4
Difficulty: Easy
Preparation Time: 10 minutes
Cook Time: 20 minutes
Total Time: 30 minutes

CITRUS COD

Ingredients

- 4 cod fillets (6 oz each weight)
- 2 tbsp. butter
- ½ cup chopped onion
- ½ tbsp. minced garlic
- 1 tsp. grated orange zest
- ¼ cup orange juice
- 1 tbsp. lemon juice
- Pinch of crushed black pepper
- 1 tbsp. minced parsley

Directions

1. Set your oven heat range to 375°F to preheat. Place fillets into the 11x7-inch baking dish sprayed with cook- ing spray. Onion and garlic should be cooked in butter over medium-high heat in a skillet until they are soft.
2. Put on top of fish. Mix orange zest and citrus juices, then drizzle over fish. Bake uncovered for 15-20 minutes or until the fish flakes apart with a fork.
3. Sprinkle crushed pepper and chopped parsley on top, serve and enjoy.

Nutrition Information:
Calories: 218kcal, Protein: 34g, Carbohydrate: 5g, Fat: 6g

Total Servings: 8
Difficulty: Medium
Preparation Time: 30 minutes
Cook Time: 10 minutes
Total Time: 40 minutes

GRILLED MAHI MAHI

Ingredients

- ¾ cup low-sodium teriyaki sauce
- 2 tbsp. sherry
- 1 tbsp. garlic cloves
- 8 mahi mahi fillets (6 oz. each weight)
- Fruit Salsa:
- 2 tbsp. extra virgin olive oil
- 1 small mango, peeled and diced
- 1 cup chopped papaya, peeled
- ¾ cup chopped green pepper
- ½ cup pineapple cubes
- ½ cup chopped red onion
- ¼ cup chopped cilantro
- ¼ cup chopped mint
- 1 tbsp. chopped jalapeno pepper
- 2 tbsp. lime juice

Directions

1. Mix the teriyaki sauce, the sherry, and the garlic in a shallow dish. Add the mahi mahi. Cover and put in the fridge for 30 minutes. In the meantime, mix the salsa ingredients in a large bowl.
2. Cover and refrigerate until serving. Drain the fillets and throw away the marinade. Put mahi mahi on a grill rack that has been oiled. Grill the covered fish over medium heat for 4–5 minutes on each side.
3. Broil it 4 inches from the heat for the same amount of time until it flakes easily with a fork. Add salsa to the dish.

Nutrition Information:
Calories: 218kcal, Protein: 32g, Carbohydrate: 9g, Fat: 6g

Total Servings: 8
Difficulty: Easy
Preparation Time: 10 minutes
Cook Time: 10 minutes
Total Time: 20 minutes

SHRIMP WITH TOMATOES & FETA

Ingredients

- 3 tbsp. olive oil
- 2 shallots, finely chopped
- 1 tbsp. minced garlic
- 6 plum tomatoes, chopped
- ½ cup chicken broth
- 1 tbsp. dried oregano
- Salt and crushed black pepper
- ¼ tsp. paprika powder
- 2 lb. shrimp, peeled and deveined
- ¾ cup crumbled feta cheese
- 2 tsp. minced fresh mint

Directions

1. In the large non-stick skillet over medium-high heat, heat the oil. Add shallots and garlic; cook, frequently stirring, until tender. Bring tomatoes, wine, oregano, salt, pepper flakes, and paprika to a boil.
2. Reduce heat; simmer for 5 minutes, uncovered. Stir in the shrimp and cheese; cook for five to six minutes or until the shrimp turn pink. Add in mint. Prepare with rice.

Nutrition Information:
Calories: 273kcal, Protein: 28g, Carbohydrate: 8g, Fat: 11g

Total Servings: 8
Difficulty: Easy
Preparation Time: 10 minutes
Cook Time: 20 minutes
Total Time: 30 minutes

PARMESAN BAKED COD

Ingredients

- 4 cod fillets (6 oz. each weight)
- ¾ cup mayonnaise
- 4 green onions, chopped
- ¼ cup grated Parmesan cheese
- 1 tsp. Worcestershire sauce

Directions

1. Preheat oven to 400 degrees Fahrenheit. Place cod in a cooking spray-coated 8-inch square baking dish. Combine the remaining ingredients and spread over the fillets. 15-20 minutes, uncovered until fish begins to flake easily with a fork.

Nutrition Information:
Calories: 299kcal, Protein: 34g, Carbohydrate: 7g, Fat: 15g

Total Servngs: 8
Difficulty: Medium
Preparation Time: 10 minutes
Cook Time: 20 minutes
Total Time: 30 minutes

FISH AND VEGGIE SKILLET

Ingredients

- 3 tbsp. olive oil, divided
- 4 salmon fillets (6 oz. each weight)
- 1 large sweet red pepper, julienned
- ½ lb. sliced baby portobello mushrooms
- 1 large, sweet onion, cut into thick rings
- ¼ cup lemon juice
- Salt and crushed place pepper
- ¼ cup chopped fresh chives
- ¼ cup pine nuts, optional

Directions

1. In a large pan, set it over medium-high heat, and warm up 2 tablespoons of oil. Add the fillets and cook for 4-5 minutes on each side or until the fish flakes apart with a fork. Take out of the pan.
2. Add the rest of the oil, the peppers, mushrooms, onion, lemon juice, and a quarter teaspoon of salt. Cover and cook over medium heat for 6–8 minutes, occasionally stirring, until the vegetables are soft.
3. Place the fish over the vegetables and sprinkle with the rest of the pepper and salt. Cover and cook for
4. about 2 minutes more, until everything is warm. Before you serve it, sprinkle it with chives and if you want, pine nuts.

Nutrition Information:
Calories: 297kcal, Protein: 35g, Carbohydrate: 10g, Fat: 13g

Total Servings: 8
Difficulty: Medium
Preparation Time: 30 minutes
Cook Time: 10 minutes
Total Time: 40 minutes

SPICY FISH PATTIES

Ingredients

- 2 whole wheat bread slices
- 2 tsp. Italian seasoning
- 2 tsp. spicy seasoning blend, without salt
- 2 large eggs, beaten
- 415g canned salmon, drained and without skin and bone
- ½ cup chopped onion
- ¼ cup chopped green pepper
- 1 tbsp. chopped jalapeno pepper
- 1 tbsp. minced garlic
- 2 tbsp. olive oil

Directions

1. Place the whole wheat bread slices with Italian seasoning and spicy seasoning blend in the food blender; cover and pulse until it turns into a fine crumb.
2. Mix the salmon, eggs, onion, green pepper, jalapeno, garlic, and ½ cup crumbs in a bowl. Make eight ½-inch thick patties. Cover with the rest of the crumbs mixture.
3. Cook patties in oil for 4-5 minutes on each side in a large non-stick skillet over medium heat. Repeat until all is done, then serve and enjoy.

Nutrition Information:
Calories 2 patties: 318kcal, Protein: 30g, Carbohydrate: 9g, Fat: 18g

Total Servings: 8
Difficulty: Easy
Preparation Time: 10 minutes
Cook Time: 20 minutes
Total Time: 30 minutes

BLACKENED TILAPIA WITH ZUCCHINI NOODLES

Ingredients

- 2 large zucchinis
- 1½ tsp. ground cumin
- Salt and crushed black pepper
- ½ tsp. smoked paprika
- ¼ tsp. garlic powder
- 4 tilapia fillets (6 oz. each weight)
- 2 tbsp. olive oil
- 1 tbsp. minced garlic
- 1 cup pico de gallo

Directions

1. Using a spiralizer, make thin zucchini noodles. Mix cumin, ½ tsp salt, smoked paprika, black pepper, and garlic powder and liberally apply to both sides of the tilapia.
2. Add oil to the non-stick skillet and put it over medium heat. Cook tilapia in batches until it flakes easily with a fork, 2 to 3 minutes per side. Remove from pan and keep warm.
3. In the same pan, cook zucchini and garlic over medium heat for 1 to 2 minutes, constantly tossing with tongs, until the zucchini is slightly softened.
4. Powder a bit of salt (if needed), then serve the fish with pico de gallo and enjoy.

Nutrition Information:
Calories: 258kcal, Protein: 34g, Carbohydrate: 8g, Fat: 10g

Total Servings: 2
Difficulty: Easy
Preparation Time: 15 minutes
Cook Time: 10 minutes
Total Time: 25 minutes

NAKED FISH TACOS

Ingredients

- 1 cup coleslaw mix
- ¼ cup chopped cilantro
- 1 green onion, sliced
- 1 tsp. chopped seedless jalapeno pepper
- 4 tsp. canola oil, divided
- 2 tsp. lime juice
- ½ tsp. ground cumin
- Salt and crushed black pepper
- 2 tilapia fillets (6 oz each)
- ½ ripe avocado, peeled and sliced

Directions

1. Put the coleslaw mix, chopped cilantro, sliced green onion, and chopped jalapeno pepper in a bowl and toss them with 2 teaspoons of oil, lime juice, cumin, 1/4 teaspoon salt, and 1/8 teaspoon of pepper. Refrigerate until serving.
2. Use paper towels to dry the fillets, then sprinkle them with the rest of the salt and pepper. Heat the rest of the oil over medium-high heat in a large non-stick skillet.
3. Cook the tilapia for 3–4 minutes per side or until the fish flakes apart easily with a fork. Add slaw and avoca-do on top.

Nutrition Information:
Calories: 300kcal, Protein: 33g, Carbohydrate: 6g, Fat: 16g

Total Servngs: 4
Difficulty: Easy
Preparation Time: 15 minutes
Cook Time: 10 minutes
Total Time: 25 minutes

COD WITH BACON & BALSAMIC TOMATOES

Ingredients

- 4 bacon strips, chopped
- 4 cod fillets (6 oz each weight)
- Salt and crushed black pepper
- 2 cups halved grape tomatoes
- 2 tbsp. balsamic vinegar

Directions

1. In a non-stick skillet, sauté bacon until it is crispy, stirring it every so often. Remove with the slotted spoon; let it drain on paper towels. Add salt and pepper to the fillets.
2. Add the fillets to the bacon grease and cook over medium-high heat for 4-6 minutes on each side or until the fish flakes apart with a fork. Remove and keep warm. Add halved tomatoes to the pan; cook and stir for 2-4 minutes until the tomatoes have softened.
3. Add the vinegar and turn the heat down to medium-low. Cook for a minute or two until the sauce has thick- ened. Serve cod with the tomato-bacon mixture.

Nutrition Information:
Calories: 216kcal, Protein: 36g, Carbohydrate: 5g, Fat: 6g

Total Servings: 2
Difficulty: Easy
Preparation Time: 10 minutes
Cook Time: 20 minutes
Total Time: 30 minutes

CILANTRO LIME SHRIMP

Ingredients

- ¼ cup chopped fresh cilantro
- 1½ tsp. grated lime zest
- ¼ cup lime juice
- 1 jalapeno pepper, seedless and minced
- 2 tbsp. olive oil
- 1 tbsp. minced garlic
- Salt and crushed black pepper
- ¼ tsp. ground cumin
- 1 lb. shrimp, peeled and deveined

Directions

1. Add chopped cilantro, zest, lime juice, jalapeno pepper, olive oil, minced garlic, ground cumin, salt, and pep- per in a bowl, then toss in shrimp. Toss them well, then set aside 15 minutes.
2. Skewer the shrimp and lime slices on either four metal or four wooden skewers that have been soaked in water. Place the shrimp over medium heat, cover the grill, and cook for 2-4 minutes per side, turning once.

Nutrition Information:
Calories: 328kcal, Protein: 38g, Carbohydrate: 8g, Fat: 16g

Total Servings: 2
Difficulty: Easy
Preparation Time: 5 minutes
Cook Time: 10 minutes
Total Time: 15 minutes

STIR-FRIED SHRIMP AND MUSHROOMS

Ingredients

- 2 tbsp. minced garlic
- 4 tsp. canola oil
- 1 lb. shrimp, peeled and deveined
- 3 cups sliced mushrooms
- 1 cup sliced green onions
- 4 tbsp. chicken broth
- Cooked Brown rice for serving
- Lemon slices for serving

Directions

1. In a large skillet or wok, sauté the garlic in the oil for one minute. Stir-fry the shrimp, mushrooms, and onions for one minute after adding them to the pan.
2. After stirring in the broth, continue cooking for two more minutes or until the shrimp have turned pink. Take the stir-fried shrimp and mushrooms with brown rice and lemon slice. Serve and enjoy.

Nutrition Information:
Calories: 296kcal, Protein: 38g, Carbohydrate: 9g, Fat: 12g

Total Servings: 4
Difficulty: Medium
Preparation Time: 5 minutes
Cook Time: 25 minutes
Total Time: 30 minutes

COD WITH SWEET PEPPERS

Ingredients

- ½ cup chopped onion
- 2 tbsp. extra virgin olive oil
- 1 cup low-sodium chicken broth
- 1 tbsp. lemon juice
- 1 tbsp. minced garlic
- 1½ tsp. dried oregano
- ½ tsp. lemon zest
- ¼ tsp. salt
- 4 cod fillets (6 oz each weight)
- ¾ cup julienned sweet red pepper
- ¾ cup julienned green pepper
- 2½ tsp. cornstarch
- 1 tbsp. cold water
- 1 lemon, halved and sliced

Directions

1. Mix the chopped onion, olive oil, chicken broth, lemon juice, minced garlic, dried oregano, and lemon zest in a large skillet that does not have a non-stick coating.
2. Bring the liquid to a boil. Turn the heat down to low, cover the pan, and simmer the onion for 6 to 8 minutes. Arrange the fish and the peppers in a pattern on top of the onion mixture.
3. Cover and keep simmering for another 6–9 minutes or until the fish is flaky and the peppers are soft. Re- move the fish and vegetables now; keep warm.
4. Mix cornstarch and water until they are smooth. Then, add them slowly to the juices in the pan. Bring to a boil and keep cooking while stirring for about 2 minutes or until the sauce has thickened.
5. Mix well and drizzle over fish and vegetables. Serve with lemon on the side.

Nutrition Information:
Calories: 253kcal, Protein: 34g, Carbohydrate: 9g, Fat: 9g

Total Servngs: 4
Difficulty: Medium
Preparation Time: 15 minutes
Cook Time: 15 minutes
Total Time: 30 minutes

ROSEMARY SALMON AND VEGGIES

Ingredients

- 1½ lb. salmon fillets, cut into 4 portions
- 2 tbsp. melted coconut oil
- 2 tbsp. balsamic vinegar
- 2 tsp. minced fresh rosemary
- ½ tbsp. minced garlic
- Salt and crushed black pepper
- 1 lb. fresh asparagus, trimmed
- 1 small sweet red pepper, chopped

Directions

1. Turn the oven up to 400°F. Lightly oil the oven sheet and put the salmon in the sheet. Mix the oil, vinegar, garlic, rosemary, and salt. Pour half over the salmon.
2. Put the asparagus and chopped red pepper in a large bowl. Drizzle the remaining oil mixture over the vege- tables and toss to coat. Sprinkle crushed pepper.
3. Bake for 12 to 15 minutes until the salmon flakes easily with a fork, and the vegetables are soft. Serve with slices of lemon.

Nutrition Information:
Calories: 359kcal, Protein: 31g, Carbohydrate: 7g, Fat: 23g

Total Servings: 4
Difficulty: Medium
Preparation Time: 10 minutes
Cook Time: 15 minutes
Total Time: 25 minutes

PEPPERED TUNA KABOBS

Ingredients

- ½ cup frozen corn, thawed
- 1 jalapeno pepper, seedless and chopped
- 4 green onions, chopped
- 2 tbsp. chopped parsley
- 2 tbsp. lime juice
- 1 lb. tuna steaks, cubed
- 1 tsp. crushed black pepper
- 2 small sweet red peppers, cubed
- 1 small mango, peeled and cubed

Directions

1. Mix the thawed corn, chopped jalapeno pepper, green onion, and chopped parsley for salsa in a small bowl and set aside.
2. Thread red peppers, tuna, and mango onto four metal or wet wooden skewers. Sprinkle crushed pepper and salt on the skewers and put the skewers on the rack of a greased grill.
3. Cook, covered, over medium heat, turning once or twice, for 10-12 minutes, or until the tuna is slightly pink in the middle (medium-rare) and the peppers are soft. Use salsa on the side.

Nutrition Information:
Calories 1 kebob: 179kcal, Protein: 29g, Carbohydrate: 9g, Fat: 3gg

Total Servings: 4
Difficulty: Hard
Preparation Time: 15 minutes
Cook Time: 30 minutes
Total Time: 45 minutes

SHRIMP AND CRABMEAT CASSEROLE

Ingredients

- 5 tbsp. unsalted butter, divided
- 32g sliced mushrooms
- 1 lb. shrimp, cooked and cut into small pieces
- 120g cooked crabmeat
- ¼ cup all-purpose flour
- 2 cups milk
- Salt and pepper as per taste
- ¼ tsp. paprika powder
- 2 tsp. sliced chives
- 2 tsp. chopped parsley
- 2 tbsp. dry white wine
- 4 tbsp. grated parmesan cheese

Directions

1. Preheat the oven to 350F. Over medium heat, melt butter (1 tbsp) in a medium saucepan or sauté pan. Add the sliced mushrooms and cook, stirring, until they are soft.
2. Put a small piece of the butter you saved on the bottom of a 1.5-quart casserole, then put the shrimp, lobster, and crabmeat in the casserole. Add the mushrooms that have been cooked.
3. Put the leftover butter in a saucepan over medium-low heat. Stir in the flour until the mixture is smooth and bubbling. Stir the food for another 2 minutes.
4. Add the milk slowly while stirring constantly. Cook and stir the sauce over low heat until it thickens and starts to bubble. Add the wine, salt, pepper, paprika, chives, and parsley.
5. Pour the sauce in slowly and mix it well with the seafood. Add parmesan cheese on top and bake for 20 minutes. Turn the broiler on for a minute to get a nice brown top. Serve right away and have fun.

Nutrition Information:
Calories: 426kcal, Protein: 47g, Carbohydrate: 10g, Fat: 22g

Total Servings: 4
Difficulty: Hard
Preparation Time: 15 minutes
Cook Time: 40 minutes
Total Time: 55 minutes

SCALLOP AND ARTICHOKE HEART CASSEROLE

Ingredients

- ½ medium artichoke hearts, cooked
- 1 lb. scallops
- 2 tbsp. avocado oil
- ¼ cup chopped red bell pepper
- ¼ cup chopped green onions
- ¼ cup almond flour
- 2 cups of low-fat milk
- 1 tsp. dried tarragon
- Salt and crushed black pepper
- 1 tbsp. chopped fresh parsley

Directions

1. Set the oven heat range to 350°F to preheat. Cut large artichoke hearts in half along their length. Set arti- choke hearts in an even layer in a square baking dish 8 inches on a side.
2. If the scallops are big, cut them in half. Spread scallops out over the artichokes. In a medium-sized non-stick saucepan, heat the oil over medium-low heat.
3. Cook and stir the bell pepper and green onions for 5 minutes or until they are soft. Mix in the flour. Add milk slowly and stir until smooth. Add the tarragon, salt, and white pepper.
4. Cook and stir over medium heat for 10 minutes or until the sauce boils and thickens. Put sauce on top of the scallops. Bake, uncovered, for about 25 minutes, or until the scallops are opaque and bubbling.
5. Garnish the dish with chopped parsley and crushed black pepper (if needed), then serve and enjoy.

Nutrition Information:
Calories: 198kcal, Protein: 20g, Carbohydrate: 7g, Fat: 10g

CONCLUSION

Research has often shown that diet is crucial when suffering from a chronic illness such as diabetes. Although there is no proper cure for diabetes, your diet plan can ease the challenging process you may be going through. Despite the restrictions, being diabetic does not imply consuming flavorless food your entire life. We assure you that you can live extraordinary lives with great food and remain healthy.

Cookbooks for people with diabetes can be a great way to enjoy delicious food while taking care of your health. They can encourage you to engage in a hobby, refine your craftsmanship, and then be able to feed yourself the food you love. Also, cookbooks can help you create recipes for your close relatives and dear ones. This, in turn, will not only keep you healthy, but the people you love will be well.

When considering cookbooks for diabetics, the essentials to ensure are the author's budget, cooking skills, time, and credibility. This is why this cookbook is perfect for you. Often, when being diagnosed with diabetes, you may feel overwhelmed and confused about what to do. Taking notes of your blood glucose level and paying attention to what to eat or not to eat can be difficult. This cookbook offers you short and quick recipes with ingredients that can be quickly bought from your local supermarket. All components are suitable for people with diabetes. When reading this cookbook, your time, budget, and skills matter to us.

The "Diabetic Cookbook For Beginners" is the top choice since it offers ideas for enjoyable, delectable, nutritionally dense meals. The author, ABC, ensures that each dish is straightforward to follow for a person of any cooking level. The dishes include 15-minute options, from breakfast to appetizers, meals, and desserts. It's always won- derful to have a picture of the cuisine you intend to prepare, and this book doesn't disappoint you with lovely images to match the recipes!

Additionally, the cookbook provides portion management for all of the enjoyable categories. This implies that you can eat it alone or with others for breakfast, supper, and snacks. There are recipes for desserts as well. Who says you cannot enjoy dessert while you have diabetes? With this cookbook, there are no limits to enjoying your favorite food.

We like that "Diabetic Cookbook For Beginners" also provides a handbook explaining how to control diabetes by consuming particular meals. You may utilize the comprehensive and simple-to-follow guidance to develop your blood sugar-balancing meals. There are two recipes on each page, providing you with abundant possibilities! The wonderful thing about "Diabetic Cookbook For Beginners" is that these meals can be made in half an hour or less while still being flavorful. Additionally, ABC begins the book with data on pre-diabetes studies, which may assist in exposing you to some of the vocabulary and suggestions crucial to understanding your illness before creating your new culinary skills!

The recipes, according to reviews, offer much of cooking ideas. Many also point out and value that the guide is appropriate for anyone who loves eating healthily, not only those with diabetes. The cookbook is for anybody who wants to eat delectable dishes while enhancing their health conditions, with recipes that allow you to go to the grocery store, acquire the goods, and get rewarded with a lovely meal within minutes.

Your path with diabetes can be difficult, but Diabetic Cookbook For Beginners cookbook can offer you a haven right in your kitchen!

Made in the USA
Las Vegas, NV
21 October 2023